Dr. med. Andreas Ganz
Bernhard Johannes Schmidt

Symbiotic Narcissism as a Group Phenomenon

Contributions to Clinical Social Psychology

Contributions to Clinical Social Psychology

Andreas Ganz
Bernhard J. Schmidt

Symbiotic Narcissism
as a
Group Phenomenon

© 2025 Bernhard J. Schmidt
Oberwarmensteinach, Germany

ISBN: 978-3-7597-8742-2

Publisher:
BoD · Books on Demand GmbH, In de Tarpen 42,
22848 Norderstedt, bod@bod.de
Print:
Libri Plureos GmbH, Friedensallee 273,
22763 Hamburg

Bibliographic information from the German National Library:
The German National Library lists this publication
in the German National Bibliography; detailed bibliographic
data are available on the Internet at http://dnb.dnb.de.

Translation of the original title
"Symbiotischer Narzissmus
als Gruppenphänomen"
(2017)

Table of content

I. INTRODUCTION

After the books on autism, we turn to more general psychological considerations in this book. We will first introduce and justify the term "clinical social psychology". This term has cropped up from time to time in the past, but without either a theoretical foundation or practical application, and has therefore not yet been able to gain acceptance.

For us, however, our work on the subject of autism has led us to "clinical social psychology". In this area, both in the development of an autism theory and practical applications, it becomes clear that the clinical side of the phenomenon of autism cannot be explained without the results of social psychology.

We will, however, limit the theoretical explanations of clinical social psychology to the bare essentials, and then turn to the topic of "symbiotic narcissism as a group phenomenon".

Here too, the practical experience of recent years, especially in dealing with parents' associations and autism researchers, has shown us the way. When looking for explanations for the consistently (!) irrational behavior of these groups, symbiotic narcissism is one possibility.

Our aim is to develop and present both the theoretical foundations and practical aspects of clinical social psychology in further volumes. We would be pleased about a constructive-critical discourse and lively participation, even if this participation would refute our hypothesis, at least in the area of autism. The hypothesis that symbiotic narcissism is the reason for the refusal to both examine the social psychological and developmental dynamic theory of autism and to discuss it.

II. CLINICAL SOCIAL PSYCHOLOGY

For us, "clinical social psychology" is the combination of clinical psychology and social psychology.

It therefore serves as a bridge that should enable exchange between the two disciplines.

Two questions need to be examined in advance:

1.) Firstly, the possibility of this combination, i.e. the question of whether there are fundamental conflicts that prevent a combination.

2.) Secondly, the question of whether a combination is theoretically and practically sensible and helpful, i.e. whether meaningful mutual influences and extensions can be assumed.

At first glance, clinical psychology, which deals primarily with psychological disorders of the individual, and social psychology, which studies the structure and behavior of groups, appear to be incompatible.

But the autism theory we have developed [Schmidt; Ganz (2016)] already shows very clearly that the psychological problems of the individual in this area cannot be understood without the results of social psychology.

On the other hand, and here we come to the topic of "symbiotic narcissism", not only are more and more people in "civilized" societies developing mental disorders,

9

but these societies themselves also seem to be "falling ill". And this can be seen primarily in politicians such as Erdogan, Trump, Johnson, Orban, etc.

But this "individualization of the irrational" to which people in general, and researchers and clinical psychologists in particular, tend, is only one side of the problem. The other side is not the politicians as individuals, however pathological their behavior may appear. The real problem is that they were elected. And, what is even worse for the prognosis, that there is often a very deep, incurable rift between supporters and opponents in the respective countries. That two irreconcilable camps are facing each other, whether Brexit, Trump, Erdogan... two sharply divided groups that are hostile to each other and that are no longer willing or able to engage in dialogue.

In addition, in affluent societies, more and more violence is being used against the police, rescue workers such as firefighters and paramedics... And this is without any understanding of or consideration for the socially relevant function of these professions. The selfish enforcement of one's own needs is increasingly not stopping at violence against those on whom one ultimately depends. And it is done without weighing up one's own short-term interests and needs against long-term ones. But the wishes and needs of other people are also not taken into account.

This makes the behavior both destructive and self-destructive.

Isolation and calls for walls, prejudice and racism ... are also increasing at an alarming rate.

As well as the increase in individual mental disorders, the European ideas of humanism and open borders are increasingly being lost.

Just as the clinical problems (clinical psychology) of autistic people can be explained by the "lack of unconscious group communication" (social psychology), in our opinion the problems described in today's societies (social psychology) can be explained by the expansion of narcissism (clinical psychology) as a "symbiotic group phenomenon".

„Der Narzissmus des Individuums läuft dem der Kultur parallel. Wir formen unsere Kultur nach unserem Bild und werden unsererseits wieder von dieser Kultur geformt. Können wir das eine ohne das andere verstehen? Kann die Psychologie die Soziologie unbeachtet lassen – oder umgekehrt?" [Lowen (1992)][1]

---

1   The narcissism of the individual runs parallel to that of culture. We shape our culture in our own image and are in turn shaped by that culture. Can we understand one without the other? Can psychology ignore sociology - or vice versa?

But culture and the individual do not just run parallel, they are mutually interwoven in their development.
We are convinced that there is nothing standing in the way of combining clinical and social psychology, but that bringing them together is necessary for understanding both the individual and problems and conflicts in society.

1   Previous applications

As already mentioned, our books on autism [Ganz; Schmidt (2016), Schmidt (2015/1, 2015/2), Schmidt; Ganz (2016)] are already contributions to clinical social psychology. Only through the results of social psychology can autism be understood as a vulnerability within a society.
The correct observations of clinical psychology that autistic people often show little facial expressions and gestures, do not imitate their counterparts, speak monotonously, etc., combined with the findings of social psychology - that people unconsciously communicate as a group and orient themselves using precisely these behaviors that autistic people often lack - lead to the conclusion that autistic people lack "unconscious group communication".
Autism is therefore not, as previously assumed, a "disorder of social interaction and communication". However,

this disorder can arise as a result of the lack of unconscious group behavior [Schmidt; Ganz (2016)].

Because of the lack of unconscious (!) group behavior, autistic people are often excluded from social interaction or withdraw from it. But social interaction is of fundamental importance for the development of all people, including autistic people [Ganz; Schmidt (2016)]. It follows that the problems frequently observed among autistic people arise from the exclusion or withdrawal from social interaction within groups, the "communities of practice" [Wenger (1998)].

It is already clear here that if clinical psychology postulates a "social" disorder, it should also use the means and insights of social psychology. At least if it wants to gain insights that go beyond those of a dyadic approach, the problems of which we will come back to later.

2   Interactions

Our approach to combining clinical and social psychology does not aim to limit one side or the other in any way or to deny its right to exist.

On the contrary, we assume that the merger into "clinical social psychology" will have positive influences on both sides and lead to constructive expansions. So, at least in our opinion, the whole of "clinical social psychology" is more than the sum of its two parts.

*„Meine These besagt, **daß Narzißmus im Einzelmenschen und in der Kultur einen gewissen Grad von Unwirklichkeit anzeigt.** Unwirklichkeit ist nicht einfach nur neurotisch, sie grenzt ans Psychotische. An einem Verhaltensmuster, das das Erringen von Erfolgen über das Bedürfnis stellt, zu lieben und geliebt zu werden, ist etwas Verrücktes. Ein Mensch, der keinen **Kontakt zur Realität** seines Wesens – zum Körper und seinen Gefühlen hat, ist etwas verrückt. Und eine Kultur, die Luft, Wasser und Erde im Namen eines »höheren« Lebensstandards verschmutzt und verseucht, hat etwas Verrücktes an sich. **Aber kann eine Kultur geisteskrank sein? Diese Vorstellung ist in der Psychiatrie keineswegs selbstverständlich. Im allgemeinen sieht man Geisteskrankheit als Kennzeichen eines Individuums an, das den Kontakt zur Realität seiner Kultur verloren hat. Nach diesem Kriterium (das seine Gültigkeit hat) ist der erfolgreiche narzißtische Mensch weit davon entfernt, geisteskrank zu sein. Es sei denn ... es sei denn, natürlich, daß der Kultur eine gewisse Geisteskrankheit innewohnt.*"
[Lowen (1992)][2]

---

2   My thesis is that narcissism indicates a certain degree of unreality in the individual and in the culture. Unreality is

Lowen describes very well the meaning of "unreality" and loss of contact with reality. But it is not only people who lose contact with reality, but also society.

The idea of a successful narcissist is wrong - it is a contradiction in terms. Although it may be possible at first, superficial glance that narcissists are successful, this is a mistake.

We will explain later why the "successful narcissist" is a contradiction in terms and why narcissism, whether in the individual or in society, is always accompanied by a deep auto-/destructive tendency. And why symbiotic narcissism can be diagnosed by this tendency. But first we want to look at the positive influences of merging the two.

---

not just neurotic, it borders on the psychotic. There is something mad about a pattern of behavior that puts the pursuit of success above the need to love and be loved. A person who is out of touch with the reality of his being - his body and his feelings - is something mad. And there is something mad about a culture that pollutes and contaminates air, water and earth in the name of a "higher" standard of living. But can a culture be insane? This idea is by no means self-evident in psychiatry. Insanity is generally seen as the mark of an individual who has lost touch with the reality of his culture. By this criterion (which is valid), the successful narcissistic person is far from being insane. Unless... unless, of course, there is some insanity inherent in the culture.

So how does the merger affect both social psychology and clinical psychology?

3 => Clinical Psychology

What effects does social psychology have on clinical psychology when it is merged into clinical social psychology? It is primarily a "mytholytic" one - it dissolves myths.

1.1 Social psychology has a mytholytic effect

Myths arise within groups and societies as shared interpretive frameworks in relation to reality. Myths are the sum of shared interpretive frameworks. They not only arise within groups and societies, they also define them. The group only includes people who have largely the same frames (interpretive frameworks), i.e. who share the same myth. Within a group or society, frames can hardly be recognized as such, because they are either perceived as "normal" or not at all. Only by comparing and examining different groups and societies with one another do their frames and myths become apparent. Clinical psychology, limited to the observation of the (sick) individual and at most a dyadic relationship, is not able to dissolve myths, i.e. to have a mytholytic effect.

3.1.a   Myth of the rational individual

In recent decades, social psychology has largely dispelled the myth of the individual through its findings, even if this is not yet perceived, cannot be or does not want to be. Even if people in individualistic cultures are reluctant to admit it, the individual and his development are very dependent on groups. On the one hand, through the conscious, but above all unconscious orientation towards the respective groups. On the other hand, through the need to participate in "communities of practice" [Wenger (1998)]. As a result, people behave to a large extent unconsciously and in a group-dependent manner [Bargh (2014), Dunning (2012)]. Due to this dependence on and orientation towards groups, people often behave not only unconsciously, but also irrationally.

„In any group of individuals that gather together for a stated purpose there will exist a conscious, task-oriented group and an underlying, unconscious group; the functioning of this underlying group may be in conflict with the requirements of the task. This is not to say that work groups never function. We meet groups for a variety of reasons – for work, politics, interest and leisure – and for the most part we manage to perform the tasks we meet to

17

achieve. However, performance may be inhibited by an-
xieties of which we may not be aware and by processes
that develop in the group in order to alleviate anxiety"
[Wetherell (1996)]

As Wetherell describes, social psychology also recogni-
zes an essential function of groups: reducing fears.
It is therefore not surprising that people adapt to groups
as a condition for participating in them.
And this is despite knowing better.

„Humans conform. With little or no reflection, we adopt
many functionless and ever-changing fads and fashions
of those around us. We not only conform to arbitrary
fashions but also conform to majority opinion when we
know better ourselves." [Haun (2011)]

3.1.b   Intrapersonal ./. Interpersonal

Another positive influence of social psychology on clinical psychology is that the understanding of the development of, for example, self-esteem is shifted from the intrapersonal to the interpersonal level [e.g. Agroskin
(2014), Lumsden (2014)].
That is, many characteristics of the individual do not arise in isolation, as is often assumed, but through interacti-

on with and dependence on the social environment. There-fore, problems of the individual often cannot be under-stood in isolation, but only by considering the interacti-ons between the individual, groups and society.

3.1.c   CRAAM dogma

It is the dogma that has shaped the self-perception of peo-ple in our culture, as well as science and philosophy, for centuries and millennia.
The idea of a "**c**onscious, **r**ational and **a**utonomously **a**cting **m**an" - the CRAAM dogma.
But social psychology shows the opposite.
For the most part, people act unconsciously, irrationally and dependently on groups. Examples include the studies by Zimbardo (Stanford Prison Experiment), Milgram (Obedience) and Tajfel (Minimal Group Paradigm). Unconscious group processes shape people and their development through imitation of and adaptation to group norms, through the development of self-esteem as an interpersonal process (Tajfel/Turner), group participation as protection against fear [Menzies Lyth (1960)] ...
This does not mean that, for example, cognitive behavi-oral therapy would not be effective for a number of men-tal disorders, but to gain a basic understanding of people and the development of mental disorders, considering the

19

conscious cognitive components is by no means suffi-cient. This must be expanded to include unconscious (group) behavior and unconscious orientation towards groups.

1.2   Expanding the dyadic perspective

Clinical psychology has so far, understandably, started from the (sick) individual, and perhaps supplemented this perspective with an asymmetrical relationship between the individual and the co-alcoholic, narcissist...
However, this overlooks the many interactions between culture as a historical process, society, groups and the in-dividual, as described, for example, by Vygotsky's "Cul-tural Historical Concept" (CHC) [Vygotsky (1929)] or Bronfenbrenner's "ecosystemic approach" [Bronfenbren-ner (1977)].
On the other hand, in addition to the dyadic and thus asymmetrical relationships between the narcissist and the co-narcissist, there are also symmetrical group relations-hips. In our understanding, two narcissists with a symme-trical (symbiotic) relationship are already a group, albeit a small one. But this group can ultimately be expanded to include almost any number of additional members. And on the other hand, it follows rules that are different from those of an asymmetric relationship.

We will return to Vygotsky and Bronfenbrenner, among others, in a later chapter.

1.3 Ending the individualization of the irrational

In current political discussions, one can clearly see the fundamental tendency to individualize irrational behavior. The focus is on one politician, be it Trump, Erdogan, Johnson..., and the large number of people who voted for them and support them are ignored.

Social psychology, on the other hand, shows that these - in our example, politicians - are only the tip of the iceberg of irrational behavior.

The combination of clinical and social psychology also opens up new perspectives on narcissism - on narcissism as a symbiotic group phenomenon.

It is also understandable that a few decades ago, when social psychology was still in its infancy, a number of phenomena were misunderstood or misinterpreted.

Erich Fromm's statements are no longer tenable from our current perspective.

„Die Frage ist nun: Können wir sicher sein, daß Menschen in ihren Beziehungen zueinander sich tatsächlich

21

als Artgenossen erleben und daher mit genetisch pro-
grammierten Verhaltensmustern auf solche Artgenossen
reagieren? Sehen wir nicht ganz im Gegenteil, daß bei
vielen primitiven Völkern selbst ein Mensch aus einem
anderen Stamm oder einer, der im Nachbardorf nur eini-
ge Meilen entfernt lebt, als ein vollkommen Fremder, ja
nicht einmal als menschliches Wesen angesehen wird,
und deshalb keine Einfühlung in ihn besteht. Erst im Pro-
zeß der sozialen und kulturellen Evolution ist die Zahl de-
rer, die als menschliche Wesen akzeptiert werden, größer
geworden. Offenbar gibt es gute Gründe für die
Annahme, ***daß der Mensch seinesgleichen nicht als Mit-***
glied derselben Spezies ansieht*, da ihm die Möglichkeit,*
den anderen als Menschen zu erkennen, nicht durch die
instinktiven, reflexähnlichen Reaktionen erleichtert wird,
mit deren Hilfe die Tiere anhand des Geruchs, der Ge-
stalt, bestimmter Farben usw. sofort den Artgenossen er-
kennen. Aus vielen Tierexperimenten geht hervor, daß
selbst das Tier bezüglich seiner Artgenossen getäuscht
oder verunsichert werden kann. Eben deshalb, weil der
Mensch, was seine Instinkte betrifft, schlechter ausgerüs-
tet ist als irgendein anderes Lebewesen, erkennt oder
identifiziert er seine Artgenossen nicht so leicht, wie Tiere
das tun. Für ihn bestimmen Sprache, Sitten, Kleidung und
andere Kriterien, die mehr geistig als instinktiv wahrge-
nommen werden, wer ein Artgenosse ist und wer nicht,

und jede Gruppe, die irgendwie anders ist, wird nicht derselben Gattung Mensch zugerechnet. Hieraus folgt das Paradoxon, daß dem Menschen, eben weil es ihm an Instinkt fehlt, auch das Erlebnis der Identität mit seinen Artgenossen abgeht und daß er den Fremden so erlebt, als ob er zu einer anderen Spezies gehörte; mit anderen Worten, es ist das Menschsein, was den Menschen so un-menschlich macht." [Fromm (1989)][3]

---

3   The question is: can we be sure that people in their relationships with one another actually experience themselves as
members of their own species and therefore react to such
members of their own species with genetically program-
med behaviour patterns? Do we not see, on the contrary,
that among many primitive peoples even a person from another tribe or one who lives in the neighbouring village only a few miles away is regarded as a complete stranger, not
even as a human being, and therefore there is no empathy
with him. It is only in the process of social and cultural
evolution that the number of those who are accepted as human beings has increased. There are evidently good reasons for assuming that man does not regard his fellow human beings as members of the same species, since the possibility of recognizing others as human beings is not facili-
tated by the instinctive, reflex-like reactions with which
animals immediately recognize members of their own species by smell, shape, certain colours, etc. Many animal experiments show that even animals can be deceived or con-

Everything stated in this quote from Fromm can now be explained more easily using the results of social psychology.

It is the unconscious group behavior through which membership in the in-group is defined and demarcation from out-groups is established.

„... *people ascribe the human essence to their ingroup and consider outgroups as less human.*" [Leyens (2003)]

Foreign groups are always perceived as inferior, they are automatically devalued, and "infrahumanization" occurs.

„*Infra-humanization, like moral exclusion, delegimization, and lesser-perceived humanity, probaly constitutes a*

---

fused about members of their own species. Precisely because man is less equipped in instinct than any other animal, he does not recognize or identify his fellow creatures as easily as animals do. For him, language, customs, dress, and other criteria, perceived more intellectually than instinctively, determine who is a fellow creature and who is not, and any group that is in any way different is not included in the same human species. Hence the paradox that, precisely because man lacks instinct, he also lacks the experience of identity with his fellow creatures and experiences strangers as if they belonged to another species; in other words, it is humanity that makes man so inhuman.

strong defense mechanism for those who want to live in a quiet environment. It explains how one can watch apartheid, wars, and genocides on TV without being too much disturbed, or having to be sent to a psychiatric hospital." [Leyens (2003)]

But if the individual orientates himself towards the group because he cannot do without this orientation due to the "unreality", the question remains: what do the groups orient themselves towards? Because, as Lowen rightly describes in the text excerpt quoted at the beginning, both the narcissistic individual and the narcissistic society are surrounded by something "unreal".

„Die andere Quelle des Gruppeneinflusses liegt in dem schon beschriebenen Bedürfnis des einzelnen, sich zu orientieren. Dies ist häufig ohne den Bezug zu Gruppenmaßstäben nicht möglich, weil wir uns die meiste Zeit nicht in einer Realität schlechthin bewegen, sondern in einer von uns oder anderen Personen geschaffenen sozialen Realität." [Thomas (1992)][4]

---

4   The other source of group influence lies in the individual's need for orientation, as already described. This is often not possible without reference to group standards, because most of the time we do not move in a reality per se, but in a social reality created by ourselves or other people.

25

And what is presented as a contradiction in the following quote by Thomas (1992), namely deindividuation on the one hand and preservation of independence on the other, can be resolved by "symbiotic narcissism as a group phenomenon".

„Deindividuation, Aufgehen in der Gruppe und individuelle Verhaltensregulation.

Die vollständige Anpassung an die soziale Umwelt, das Aufgehen in einer Gruppe, die ent-individualisierte Integration in ein Team einerseits und andererseits die Entwicklung, Aufrechterhaltung und Verteidigung der individuellen Identität, **die Glorifizierung individueller Leistungsfähigkeit, Eigenständigkeit und Macht** sowie das Bestreben, sich in seiner Eigenständigkeit deutlich von anderen Menschen abzuheben, Distanz zu halten, stellen **ein unauflösliches Dilemma** menschlicher Existenz dar. Unter Deindividuation wird ein Zustand verstanden, in dem eine Person in ihrem Denken, Empfinden und Handeln sich so weit den Anforderungen durch eine Gruppe anpaßt und dem Druck bzw. den Attraktionen von Masse und Kollektiv so weit folgt, daß die intrapersonalen Handlungsregulatoren, z. B. die Orientierung an internalisierten Werten und Normen, bedeutungslos *werden im Vergleich zur Übermacht externaler Handlungsdeterminanten."* [Thomas (1992)][5]

The advantages of the merger lie both in the mytholytic effect and in the expansion of an individual/dyadic perspective towards the consideration of the interactions between individuals, groups and society.

---

5   Deindividuation, merging into the group and individual behaviour regulation. The complete adaptation to the social environment, merging into a group, the de-individualised integration into a team on the one hand and on the other hand the development, maintenance and defence of the individual identity, the glorification of individual performance, independence and power as well as the striving to clearly distinguish oneself from other people in one's independence and to keep one's distance represent an insoluble dilemma of human existence. Deindividuation is understood as a state in which a person adapts his thinking, feelings and actions to the demands of a group and follows the pressure or attractions of the mass and collective to such an extent that the intrapersonal action regulators, e.g. the orientation towards internalised values and norms, become insignificant compared to the overwhelming power of external action determinants.

1.4   => Social psychology

What effects would a connection to "clinical social psychology" have on social psychology?

The advantages lie primarily in the expansion of explanatory approaches.

For example, the study of autistic people shows that constructs such as conformity, imitation, obedience, self-stereotyping... are much more complex than previously assumed [e.g. Yafai et al. (2014)].

In the area of narcissism, the integration of the clinical perspective into a "symbiotic narcissism as a group phenomenon" also makes the structures and developments of groups and societies more understandable and, to a certain extent, predictable.

We will make a comparison later between the construct of the "narcissistic personality" in clinical psychology and the "authoritarian personality" in social psychology.

3.1.d   Excursus: Ambivalence of Borders

When looking at boundaries nowadays, we often only see their restrictive effect. The so-called individual and society consciously strive to overcome boundaries.

In modern child-rearing, setting boundaries, often combined with one or another, more or less friendly exercise of power, is seen as negative and counterproductive.

But boundaries do not just restrict, they also offer security and definition.

That is why children who are no longer given boundaries lack security and the opportunity to understand and discover the world within manageable boundaries. But adults also need boundaries. The idea of boundlessness is misleading - and then leads to the opposite call that we can observe within today's societies, the call for boundaries, walls, fences. For cultural "identity", i.e. demarcation from other cultures. As in many other areas, the measure is crucial when it comes to boundaries. So boundaries that provide sufficient security without being too restrictive are sensible and necessary.

4   Precursor

Having established that there are no fundamental contradictions to a connection between clinical and social psychology, and that this connection would have positive effects on both sides, we now want to look at some of the forerunners and pioneers of "clinical social psychology". When assessing these predecessors, it must always be remembered that social psychology either did not exist at all or was still in its infancy at the time. And "unconscious group behavior" in particular had not yet been researched to the extent that it is today.

1.5   Adler

What is particularly interesting about Alfred Adler is that he started with an individual, "solipsistic" approach. Even in the "Study on the Inferiority of Organs" [referred to as "the study" in the quotations], Adler takes an individual approach.

„Trotzdem gilt auch für den Ansatz der 'Studie', dass darin das Subjekt mit seinen Organen allein ist. Er ist, wie der Freudsche, ein solipsistischer, ein sozial-atomistischer Ansatz, ein Ansatz, der den Menschen beschreibt, ohne einen Blick auf die Tatsache zu werfen, dass seine Existenz "ihrem innersten Wesen nach das Leben mit und für den Mitmenschen ist" (Harvey Cox).“
[Vorwort zu Adler (1977)][6]

---

6   Nevertheless, the approach of the 'study' is also true of the fact that the subject is alone with his organs. Like Freud's, it is a solipsistic, social-atomistic approach, an approach that describes man without taking a look at the fact that his existence "is, in its innermost essence, life with and for his fellow man" (Harvey Cox).

But breaking away from Freud, among others, Adler developed a social-dynamic approach.

„In den fünf Jahren zwischen 'Studie' und 'Nervösen Charakter' findet nun eine Entwicklung statt, an deren Ende die Szene völlig verändert ist.

... Im Mittelpunkt der Betrachtungen standen früher Organe zwischen anderen Organen an einer bestimmten Stelle im Organismus und mit einer bestimmten Funktion in ihm. Jetzt finden wir an deren Stelle Menschen zwischen anderen Menschen, an einer bestimmten Stelle und mit einer bestimmten Rolle in Gebilden, die selbst aus lebenden Menschen bestehen, und mit bestimmten Spannungen und Tendenzen zwischen ihnen.“

[Vorwort zu Adler (1977)][7]

---

7   In the five years between 'Study' and 'Nervous Character' a development takes place at the end of which the scene is completely changed.

... The focus of the observations used to be organs between other organs, in a certain place in the organism and with a certain function in it. Now in their place we find people between other people, in a certain place and with a certain role in structures which themselves consist of living people, and with certain tensions and tendencies between them.

It is therefore the interactions and relationships between the individual and the group on which the manifestation of a mental illness depends – via a "position effect".

„Auch die körperliche Beeinträchtigung wirkt neurose-erzeugend nur auf dem Umweg über ihren Positionsef-fekt, als Anlass einer erlebten Unterlegenheit im Ver-gleich mit anderen.

... Voll verständlich wird dies erst durch die Klärung einer weiteren Bedeutung von 'Position'. Sie bedeutet nämlich nicht nur eine bestimmte Stelle in einem Koordi-natensystem, sondern außerdem **eine Zugehörigkeit oder Nichtzugehörigkeit zu einer Gruppe – und zu den ande-ren überhaupt -, das Innerhalb- oder Außerhalbsein, das Aufgenommen- oder Isoliertsein.** *Diese beiden Posi-tionen sind zwei Verhaltensweisen des Menschen zuge-ordnet, die man am besten mit einem Ausdruck der ver-gleichenden Verhaltensforschung als* **"Freundverhalten"** *und* **"Feindverhalten"** *bezeichnet."*
[Vorwort zu Adler (1977)][8]

---

8 Even physical impairment only causes neurosis indirectly via its position effect, as a reason for an experienced inferi-ority in comparison with others.
... This only becomes fully understandable when another meaning of 'position' is clarified. It does not only mean a specific place in a coordinate system, but also belonging or

What is referred to in the previous quote as "friend behavior" and "enemy behavior" from behavioral research can now be better explained by social psychology's research into "in-group" and "out-group" behavior. Above all, this also makes clear the (often unconscious) processes that lead to belonging or exclusion.

[*The following texts about Vygotsky and Bronfenbrenner are largely taken from the book "Schmidt; Döhler; Döhler: Autism – Sexuality – Partnership" (2018).*]

1.6   Vygotsky

Vygotsky's cultural historical concept is particularly designed for (educational) use during education of disabled children. In his book "Fundamentals of Defectology" [Vygotsky (1929)], therefore, Vygotsky focuses on comparing various educational approaches.
Building on Alfred Adler and William Stern, Vygotsky pays particular attention to the interaction between

---

not belonging to a group - and to the others in general -, being inside or outside, being accepted or isolated. These two positions are associated with two types of human behavior that are best described using a term from comparative behavioral research as "friend behavior" and "enemy behavior."

disabled children and the cultural environment. In doing so, he mainly focuses on blind and deaf-dumb children, as well as children with intellectual disabilities.

„It is self-explanatory that blindness and deafness are biological factors, and in no way social. The fact of the matter is that education must cope not so much with these biological factors as with their social consequences. When we have before us a blind child as a subject for education, then we have to deal not so much with blind-ness by itself as with those conflicts which face the blind child on his entrance into the world. At that time, all the systems which determine the child's social behavior are disrupted. And therefore, it seems to me from a pedagogi-cal point of view, the education of such a child amounts to rectifying completely these social ruptures.“
 [Vygotsky (1929)]

Vygotsky is convinced that instead of asking "What disease/disability does the person have?", one must ask the questions: "Which person has the disease/disability?" and "In what and through what socio-cultural environ-ment did the disease/disability arise?"

„More simply speaking, from both the psychological and the pedagogical points of view the question has commonly been posed in crude physical and medical terms.
A physical handicap has been analysed and compensated for as just that, a handicap.
Blindness has been defined as simply the absence of sight, deafness the absence of hearing, as if we were dealing with a blind dog or a deaf jackal. In addition to that, we have lost sight of the fact that, in contrast with the case of animals, a physical handicap in a human being can never affect the personality directly because the eye and ear of a human being are not only physical organs but also social organs, because between the world and a human being stands his social environment, which refracts and guides everything proceeding from man to the world and from the world to man. Human beings do not have simple, asocial, direct communication with the world.
A loss of vision or hearing means, therefore, first and foremost the failure of serious social functions, the degeneration of societal ties, and the disruption of all behavioral systems.
In psychology and pedagogy, the problem of a child's handicap must be posed and comprehended as a social problem, because the social aspect, which formerly went unnoticed and was usually considered secondary, in fact,

*turns out to be paramount and central. This must be pla-
ced at the head of our list. We must boldly look at this
social problem as such, straight on.*" [Vygotsky (1929)]

What is sometimes hotly debated today in the area of
demanding and promoting inclusion can already be found
in Vygotsky's work at the end of the 1920s.
It must be remembered that at the time of Vygotsky neit-
her social psychology existed as a discipline, let alone the
current research results on unconscious group behavior.

1.7   Bronfenbrenner

If development is understood as a reciprocal interaction
between the individual and the socio-cultural environment, including feedback, then the individual-dyadic
approach, still in use in autism research today, is simply
inadequate. Bronfenbrenner's ecosystem approach is
infinitely better suited to the problem.
Bronfenbrenner worked for a time with Leontiev, a stu-
dent of Vygotsky, and bases his approach on Vygotsky's
cultural historical concept.

„*The entire psychological life of an individual consists of
a succession of combative objectives, directed at the reso-
lution of a single task: to secure a definite position with*

respect to the immanent logic of human society, or to the demands of the social environment. In the last analysis, the fate of personality is decided not by the existence of a defect in itself but by its social consequences, by its socio-psychological realization. In connection with this, it becomes necessary for the psychologist to understand each psychological act not only with respect to the past but also in conjunction with the future direction of personality." [Vygotsky (1929)]

Unlike Vygotsky, who focused largely on pedagogical applications, Bronfenbrenner developed a research method:

„*Definition 1. The ecology of human development is the scientific study of the progressive, mutual accommodation, throughout the life span, between a growing human organism and the changing immediate environments in which it lives, as this process is affected by relations obtaining within and between these immediate settings, as well as the larger social contexts, both formal and informal, in which the settings are embedded.*" [Bronfenbrenner (1977)]

In particular, Bronfenbrenner wishes to supplement laboratory research with field studies, as these are more true

37

to life. His characterization of developmental psychology based solely on laboratory experiments is caustic:

„From this perspective, it can be said that much of contemporary developmental psychology is the science of the strange behavior of children in strange situations with strange adults for the briefest possible periods of time.“ [Bronfenbrenner (1977)]

It is fair to say that clinical psychology is often not much different at present. (Sick) individuals are assessed and treated in unnatural environments in the shortest possible time.
In addition, Bronfenbrenner has already pointed out that limiting ourselves to dyadic processes is not enough to understand human behavior and human development.

„“... the understanding of human development demands going beyond the direct observation of behavior on the part of one or two persons in the same place; it requires examination of multiperson systems of interaction not limited to a single setting and must take into account aspects of the environment beyond the immediate situation containing the subject.“ [Bronfenbrenner (1977)]

Unfortunately, a comprehensive representation of Bronfenbrenner's approach would take too long. We refer you to the literature notes in the appendix, and quote a quick summary from www.wikipedia.com:

"An ecosystem is a community of living organisms in conjunction with the nonliving components of their environment.
Ecology is the scientific analysis and study of interactions among organisms and their environment.
A system is a regularly interacting or interdependent group of items forming a unified whole.

This system is composed of five socially organized subsystems that support and guide human development:

Microsystem
Refers to the institutions and groups that most immediately and directly impact the child's development including: family, school, religious institutions, neighbourhood, and peers.

Mesosystem
Interconnections between the microsystems, Interactions between the family and teachers, Relationship between the child's peers and the family

Exosystem

Involves links between a social setting in which the individual does not have an active role and the individual's immediate context. For example, a parent's or child's experience at home may be influenced by the other parent's experiences at work. The parent might receive a promotion that requires more travel, which might increase conflict with the other parent and change patterns of interaction with the child.

Macrosystem

Describes the culture in which individuals live. Cultural contexts include developing and industrialized countries, socioeconomic status, poverty, and ethnicity. A child, his or her parent, his or her school, and his or her parent's workplace are all part of a large cultural context. Members of a cultural group share a common identity, heritage, and values. The macrosystem evolves over time, because each successive generation may change the macrosystem, leading to their development in a unique macrosystem.

Chronosystem

The patterning of environmental events and transitions over the life course, as well as sociohistorical circumstances. For example, divorces are one transition.

Researchers have found that the negative effects of divorce on children often peak in the first year after the divorce. By two years after the divorce, family interaction is less chaotic and more stable. An example of sociohistorical circumstances is the increase in opportunities for women to pursue a career during the last thirty years."

If this ecosystem model is taken as a base, it is immediately clear that limiting observation solely to one's own culture limits and distorts the knowledge gained. Without culture-spanning social psychology, many behaviours appear, on the macrosystem level, to be absolute and fixed. Not, as is actually the case, as relative, changeable, and dependent on culture, but rather as always valid.

1.8   Cross-cultural social psychology

Unlike social psychology, which looks at group processes and interactions within a social macrosystem and uncovers and examines unconscious group behavior, for example, cross-cultural social psychology compares different social macrosystems, as well as their values and the behavior of groups and individuals within them. And just as social psychology has a mytholytic effect on the level of supposedly conscious, rational and autonomous behavior, cross-cultural social psychology has this effect on emotions, for example, how they are perceived and shown.

4.1.a   Mytholytic Effect II

Many behaviors and characteristics are transmitted through (unconscious) learning processes within a culture. If you look at the evaluation of events (event appraisal), which emotions arise in a situation and how they are shown, but also which gender roles men and women take on, ... these appear to be static and unconditional because they are very uniform due to the cultural conditioning within a culture. However, if you compare social macrosystems with each other, as cross-cultural social psychology does, it quickly becomes clear how dependent many behaviors and characteristics of the individual are on the cultural context.

We cannot reproduce this research area in full here, but would like to refer you to the book by Smith and Bond "Social Psychology Across Cultures".

In this book, among other things, it is described in detail how different the following points are in different cultures:

- *Partner preferences*
- *Gender stereotypes*
- *Decoding emotions*

- *Experiencing emotions*
- *Showing emotions*
- *Event appraisal and emotions*
- *Explaining the causes of others' behavior*
- *Choosing what we strive for*
- *Self-esteem*
- *Subjective well-being*
- *Perceived quality of life*
[Smith, Bond (1998)]

As an example, we will briefly discuss the *Event apprai-sal and emotions.*

4.1.b   Event appraisal and emotions

Without cross-cultural social psychology, it is easy to suppose that we can only react to events emotionally. But even our emotional reaction to an event and our determination as to whether the emotional feeling is socially acceptable is influenced by our culture.

„*Culture then exercises a decisive influence on the emoti-on experienced by shaping how a given event is interpre-ted or appraised. So, if one is socialized to believe that one could have controlled a negative outcome, one might feel guilty. If different cultural training led one to percei-*

ve that exercising control was impossible, then one might instead feel sad. Culture will also shape whether people evaluate the resultant emotional feeling as socially acceptable or not. ... Finally, cultures will influence the way in which the emotion is displayed and responded to in a given situation (Mesquita and Frijda, 1992)."
[Smith, Bond (1998)]

In summary, it must be stated that research approaches to emotions - not only in autistic people - must go beyond individual/dyadic approaches if they are to lead to groundbreaking results.
And it also becomes clear again that socio-emotional development takes place within a socio-cultural environment and therefore this environment must be taken into account.

5 Summary

So far we have shown that there are no contradictions in the connection between clinical and social psychology to form "clinical social psychology" and that this connection can have positive effects and extensions for both disciplines. The example of autism research makes it clear that the phenomenon of autism as vulnerability within a socio-cultural context can only be understood and researched by combining the clinical symptoms on the one hand with the results of social psychology on the other. The problems resulting from vulnerability can also only be understood and treated within clinical social psychology. It is the interaction between the individual and groups that can lead to problems. It is not just the autistic person who withdraws from interaction, it is also groups that exclude autistic people and prevent them from participating in the "communities of practice" [Wenger (1998)]. In this way, autistic people are denied the basic conditions for healthy development.

III. NARCISSISM

After the basic considerations of clinical social psychology, we now turn to the consideration of narcissism. Here, as with the autism theory, we again apply the connection between clinical and social psychology.

If we accept both that narcissism is a defining element of our current society and the interactions between society and the individual, then the new perspective offers important impulses for understanding narcissistic disorders not only in the individual, but also in society as a whole.

1   Age of Narcissism

Every era has its own structure and the mental disorder that fits that structure. This disorder does not necessarily have to be the most common, nor the one with the most tragic consequences... but it is the one that fits the structure of society best and therefore receives the most attention. In the Victorian era, the structure was primarily characterized by prudishness and the repression of sexuality. As a result of this, among other things, hysteria was the mental disorder that was the focus of interest.

„Gesellschaftliche Einflüsse: Jede Epoche entwickelt ihre eigenen, besonderen Krankheitsbilder, die in übertriebener Form die zugrundeliegenden Charakterstruktur zum Ausdruck bringen. Zu Zeiten Freuds steigerten Hysterie und Zwangsneurosen jene Charakterzüge ins Extrem, die mit der kapitalistischen Gesellschaftsordnung in einer früheren Phase ihrer Entwicklung verbunden waren: Habsucht, fanatischer Arbeitseifer und eine harte Unterdrückung der Sexualität.“ [Lasch (1980)][9]

After the World War, Lasch describes, the picture changed towards a narcissistic basic structure of society and narcissistic personality disorders among people.

„»Was die Hysterie und die Zwangsneurosen... zu Beginn dieses Jahrhunderts für Freud und seine frühen Kollegen waren«, notiert Michael Beldoch, »sind für den praktischen Analytiker der letzten Jahrzehnte vor der Jahrtausendwende die narzißtischen Störungen. Die heutigen Pa-

---

9   Social influences: Every era develops its own particular clinical pictures, which express the underlying character structure in an exaggerated form. In Freud's time, hysteria and obsessional neuroses exaggerated those character traits that were associated with the capitalist social order in an earlier phase of its development: greed, fanatical work ethic and a harsh repression of sexuality.

*tienten leiden im großen und ganzen nicht an hysteri-
schen Paralysen der Beine oder an Waschzwängen; statt
dessen ist bei ihnen das psychische Ich empfindungslos
geworden, das müssen sie immer wieder bürsten, in einem endlosen, erschöpfenden Mühen, sauber zu werden.«
Diese Patienten klagen über das »alles beherrschende
Gefühl von Leere und eine tiefe Störung ihrer Selbstach-
tung«."* [Lasch (1980)][10]

The "disorder" that receives the most attention in our
time is not narcissism - but autism. And this increased,
even exaggerated attention can be found in both the
media and in research. Autism is the dominant topic of
our time and is also the colorful carousel on the fair-
ground of vanity. For decades, several tens of thousands
of studies on the subject of autism have been published

---

10 "What hysteria and obsessional neuroses... were for Freud
    and his early colleagues at the beginning of this century,"
    notes Michael Beldoch, "narcissistic disorders are for the
    practical analyst of the last decades before the turn of the
    millennium. Today's patients do not, by and large, suffer
    from hysterical paralysis of the legs or from obsessions
    with washing; instead, their psychic ego has become insen-
    sitive, and they must brush it again and again in an endless,
    exhausting effort to become clean." These patients com-
    plain of the "all-pervading feeling of emptiness and a pro-
    found disturbance of their self-esteem."

every year, but no new knowledge has been gained. We go around in circles with the same colorful "theories" that keep cropping up just as regularly as the fire engine, the horse, car and motorcycle on the children's carousel.

2   Individual

Let us first turn to the appearance of narcissism in the individual, even though it has already been described in detail. However, we would like to add here some key points for understanding it, especially in relation to groups and society as symbiotic narcissism.

1.9   Unreality

The basic problem with narcissists is the need for revaluation, i.e. the appreciation of one's own person and the devaluation of the environment.

„Generally speaking, narcissism (from an analytical perspective) is a reaction to the fear of losing a loved reference object that has already been experienced and is therefore feared again in the future. A strong personality architecture (i.e. usually an already differentiated and adult P) can allow this fear, and if necessary also show it appropriately to the outside world and deal with it.

A weaker personality, for example a child in its early development phase, perceives this loss as an existential threat that it cannot counteract. In order to deal with this indirectly (= neurotically), it begins to devalue the reference object a priori and to increase its value in order to keep the damage to itself as low as possible in the event of a loss of the relationship." [Schmidt; Ganz (2016)]

This psychological need for revaluation results above all in fear of reality, because direct contact with reality would prove the revaluation to be an illusion. In addition to or because of the need to increase the value of oneself and devalue the environment, the narcissistic person has a disturbed relationship to the environment and reality.

*„In dem Maße, wie ein Mensch narzißtisch ist, hat er einen doppelten Maßstab für seine Wahrnehmungen. Nur er selbst und was zu ihm gehört, besitzt Signifikanz, während die übrige Welt mehr oder weniger ohne Gewicht und Farbe ist, und ein narzißtischer Mensch weist aufgrund dieses doppelten Maßstabs **schwere Defekte in seinem Urteilsvermögen und seiner Fähigkeit zur Objektivität** auf.*" [Fromm (1989)][11]

---

11 To the extent that a person is narcissistic, he has a double standard for his perceptions. Only he himself and what belongs to him has significance, while the rest of the world

The environment presents two profound problems for narcissists.

Firstly, the environment is constantly changing and thereby causes new fears.

Secondly, contact with reality is both a measure and a control for one's own (inflated) self-esteem.

In order to achieve security and to be able to maintain one's own inflated self-esteem, ideologies are the means of choice, and not only for narcissists.

„Noch fester fasst der Nervöse seinen Gott, sein Idol, sein Persönlichkeitsideal ins Auge und klammert sich an seine Leitlinie, verliert dabei mit tieferer Absicht die Wirklichkeit aus dem Auge, während der Gesunde stets bereit ist, dieses Hilfsmittel, diese Krücke aufzugeben und unbefangen mit der Realität zu rechnen. Der Neurotiker gleicht in diesem Falle einem Menschen, der zu Gott aufschaut, ihm seine Wege empfiehlt und nun gläubig harrt, wie der Herr es lenken werde; er ist ans Kreuz seiner Fiktion geschlagen. Auch der Gesunde kann und wird sich seine Gottheit schaffen, sich nach oben gezogen fühlen, wird aber nie die Wirklichkeit aus dem Auge verlieren und mit

---

is more or less without weight and color, and a narcissistic person, because of this double standard, has serious defects in his judgment and ability to be objective.

ihr seine Rechnung machen, sobald es aufs Wirken und Schaffen ankommt. " [Adler (1977)][12]

2.1.a   Excursus: Ideology

What characterizes an ideology? How can you identify and differentiate between them?

According to our definition, an ideology is above all an "exclusive promise of salvation".
The focus of an ideology is always a promise of salvation. This means that if you follow the instructions and rules contained in the ideology, this will lead to "salvation", whatever that may look like. Be it the salvation of "paradise", the "72 virgins", "eternal health and youth" as

---

12 The nervous person focuses even more firmly on his God, his idol, his personality ideal and clings to his guiding principles, losing sight of reality with a deeper intention, while the healthy person is always ready to give up this aid, this crutch, and to deal with reality without prejudice. In this case, the neurotic is like a person who looks up to God, recommends his ways to him and then waits in faith to see how the Lord will guide him; he is nailed to the cross of his fiction. The healthy person can and will create his own deity, feel himself drawn upwards, but will never lose sight of reality and reckon with it as soon as it comes to working and creating.

a modern replacement for "eternal life", ...

And an ideology is always "exclusive" in that it inherently conveys that only this one path leads to "salvation" – and all other paths automatically lead to ruin.

Only this one diet makes you slim, only this one belief is the path to paradise (which is why ecumenism will hardly be able to work) ...

An ideology must be followed uncritically, alternatives must not even be considered.

An ideology always presents itself as the only possible way and prohibits and prevents critical thinking.

In order to implement and enforce "exclusivity", an external "enemy" is always needed, against whom one can distance oneself and who must be fought. The destructive intolerance towards other approaches and people who think differently usually leads to excessive violence against them.

„Die «erfolgreiche» Fahndung nach Hexen, deren durch Folter erpreßten Geständnisse und die spektakulären Verbrennungen konnten die Illusion vermitteln, sämtliche Leid verursachenden Übel mit den Hexen allmählich austreiben zu können. Wenn auch Papst Innozenz VIII. von Hexen beiderlei Geschlechts sprach und wenn gelegentlich der Hexenjagd auch Männer zum Opfer fielen, konzentrierte sich die Projektion doch weit überwiegend auf

Frauen. … Inzwischen gibt es zwar längst keine Hexenprozesse mehr. aber in zahlreichen Abkömmlingen manifestiert sich weiterhin die Tendenz, Leiden schlechthin durch Anprangerung und Vernichtung von verteufelten Außenfeinden zu beseitigen. … Es ist indessen irreführend, die Leidensabwehr durch Außenprojektion lediglich in solchen furchtbaren Extremvarianten zu suchen: Schließlich gehört das zugrunde liegende Reaktionsmuster zu den verbreitetsten Bewältigungstechniken des alltäglichen Lebens. " [Richter (1982)][13]

---

13 The "successful" search for witches, their confessions extracted through torture and the spectacular burnings were able to convey the illusion that all the evils that caused suffering could be gradually expelled with the help of witches. Even though Pope Innocent VIII spoke of witches of both sexes and even though men occasionally fell victim to the witch hunt, the projection was still concentrated predominantly on women. … There have long been no witch trials, but in many descendants the tendency to eliminate suffering in general by denouncing and destroying demonized external enemies continues to manifest itself. … However, it is misleading to look for the defense against suffering through external projection only in such terrible extreme variants: after all, the underlying reaction pattern is one of the most common coping techniques in everyday life.

An ideology serves to ward off suffering by drawing rigid and far too narrow boundaries, by eliminating criticism and by distancing oneself from and showing intolerance towards outsiders.

An ideology offers a supposed sense of security and orientation because it always claims that it is the only one that leads to the goal, that complicated, critical and unsettling considerations and deliberations are unnecessary.

Ideologies and ideologists can be found in all areas - alongside non-ideological elements. They can be found in religions, in politics and science, in the health sector... and are generally good business.

The definition of ideology as an "exclusive promise of salvation" enables the distinction to be made between, for example, the ideological and theological part of a religion, the ideological and rational part of health care, politics...

For example, Islamist terror as an ideology that is always destructive can be distinguished, at least theoretically, from the religious side of Islam.

Ideologies give their followers an uncritical sense of belonging to a group, and a feeling of belonging to the "chosen ones" on the one hand.

And above all, they offer simple answers to complex human problems.

And, like narcissism, they always have a destructive effect. And this regardless of the theoretical "justificati-on" used, which is ultimately interchangeable.

1.10   Avoidance of change

Change is always a path into the unknown and therefore causes fear. For narcissists, however, change is perceived as even more threatening because the change could jeo-pardize their own self-esteem. Change always includes the possibility of failure.
Socrates is credited with the following saying:

The secret of change is to focus all your energy not on fighting the old, but on building the new.

With narcissists, however, the opposite can be observed. They fight the old with the same fierce intensity as they fear the new. It is the fake and mirror fights that characte-rize narcissistic behavior. In a world full of people and therefore full of mistakes and errors, there are any num-ber of things that can be fought against. And with almost no risk of anything changing.

1.11   Ignoring

In order to secure the narcissistic self-perception, the environment, because it serves as a benchmark, must be ignored with all its facets.

different levels of competence

In many areas today, people's perceptions ignore different levels of competence. Scientists and specialists who have spent their entire lives intensively dealing with a topic are not perceived as more competent in any way. On the contrary, the "Dunning-Kruger effect" is increasingly common. This postulates that as competence decreases, the means of perceiving the lack of competence also become less and less.

This means that the less people know about a subject, the more competent they consider themselves to be.

As a result, competences as well as scientific principles and results are not recognized - and often mutually, which then leads to a fruitless exchange that does not deserve the name of dialogue or discourse.

reality

Ultimately, reality as a whole is ignored or interpreted arbitrarily. We live in a post-factual society with "alternative facts". Narcissists live in a Pippi Longstocking idyll of "I make the world the way I like it".
As a result, a key characteristic of narcissists is that they are largely resistant to advice. Advice does not just mean confronting reality, but also the threat of a process that is supposed to lead to change.

„Auch die notwendigen Einschränkungen durch die Wirklichkeit, wo sich hart im Raume die Dinge stoßen, drängen ihn gemäß seiner Einstellung nicht zur Beseitigung der vorgefaßten Fiktion, sondern nur zur seiner Wandlung ins Pessimistische. Noch konsequenter versucht der psychotische Patient die Realisierung seiner Fiktion durchzusetzen. Der Neurotiker zappelt im Realen an seiner selbstgeschaffenen Leitlinie und gelangt dadurch zu einer scheinbaren Spaltung seiner Persönlichkeit, dass er der realen und imaginären Forderung gerecht werden will, um durch diesen Zweifel zu bremsen und ihn im stecken zu bleiben." [Adler (1977)][14]

---

14 Even the necessary limitations imposed by reality, where
    things collide in space, do not force him to eliminate the

1.12   (auto-)destructive structures

If reality is perceived as a threat and change is feared, then an important question for understanding the narcissistic personality is how the human need for "effectiveness" [Wirkmächtigkeit] can be satisfied at all.

"Der Mensch kann von der Liebe oder von der Leidenschaft getrieben werden, zu zerstören; in beiden Fällen befriedigt er eines seiner existentiellen Bedürfnisse: das Bedürfnis, etwas zu »bewirken«, jemand zu bewegen." [Fromm (1989)][15]

---

preconceived fiction, but only to transform it into pessimism, in accordance with his attitude. The psychotic patient tries even more consistently to implement the realization of his fiction.

The neurotic fidgets with his self-created guideline in reality and thereby comes to an apparent split in his personality, in that he wants to do justice to the real and imaginary demands, only to be slowed down by this doubt and to get stuck in the process.

15   Man can be driven by love or by the passion to destroy; in both cases he satisfies one of his existential needs: the need to "make something happen", to move someone.

We already mentioned at the beginning that it is the destructive action structures that can be used to identify narcissism. Incapable of constructive action in reality, it is the destructive actions that do not require any skills that satisfy the need for effectiveness.

To build a wall, you need practice and skills, and you can fail at them.
To tear down a wall, on the other hand, all you need is a sledgehammer.
Destructiveness in narcissists is not only observable in external relationships, but is also directed against them, and in two areas.
Firstly, through self-destructive behavior such as drug or alcohol addiction.
On the other hand, the need to defend against threatening events or critical people is so strong that they fight them with all their might - even if the resulting damage to themselves is many times greater than that of the opponent.
The (auto)destructive behavior becomes particularly severe when narcissism is violated.

„Wenn andere seinen Narzißmus verletzen, indem sie ihn geringschätzig behandeln, ihn kritisieren und bloßstellen, weil er etwas Falsches gesagt hat, wenn sie ihn beim

Spiel schlagen oder bei zahlreichen anderen Gelegenheiten kränken, dann reagiert ein solcher narzißtischer Mensch gewöhnlich mit intensivem Zorn oder mit Wut, ob er es nun zeigt oder nicht. Es kommt sogar vor, daß er sich dessen selber nicht bewußt ist. Wie intensiv diese aggressive Reaktion oft sein kann, zeigt sich daran, daß ein solcher Mensch jemandem, der seinen Narzißmus verwundet hat, dies niemals verzeiht und daß sein Rachedurst oft größer ist, als wenn ihn jemand körperlich verwundet oder um sein Eigentum gebracht hätte."
[Fromm (1989)][16]

A central and important problem with narcissists is the narcissism trap. Narcissists can hardly change their behavior because change is perceived as dangerous and threatening. This also means that personality development is

---

16 When others hurt his narcissism by treating him with contempt, criticizing and humiliating him for saying something wrong, beating him at play, or hurting him on numerous other occasions, such a narcissistic person usually reacts with intense anger or rage, whether he shows it or not. He may even be unaware of it himself. The intensity of this aggressive reaction can often be seen in the fact that such a person never forgives someone who has wounded his narcissism, and that his thirst for revenge is often greater than if someone had physically wounded him or robbed him of his property.

almost impossible. The ability to forgive insults, e.g. through criticism, is also necessary for personality development. But this is largely lacking in narcissists.

1.13   Communication

The need to avoid contact with reality as a measure of self-worth and to avoid fear-inducing changes, while at the same time satisfying the need for effectiveness, naturally also has a (negative) effect on the communication structure of narcissists.

Communication is a form of interaction with reality (perceived as threatening).

No discussion on the substantive level

If one distinguishes between factual and relational levels in communication, it is clear that narcissists are hardly capable of discourse on the factual level, at least in relevant aspects. Because the debate on the factual level involves critical contact with reality as a measure of one's own actions. Therefore, an attack or a shift to the relational level usually occurs.

It is not the (controversial) issue or theory that is criticized, but the person(s) who represent it. Not only is a statement or criticism not evaluated independently of the speaker, but on the contrary, only the opponent as a person is usually discredited and attacked.

The result is a personalization instead of differentiation of criticism and problems - and this is sometimes tangible, as was the case at Donald Trump's [first] election rallies, where critics were also knocked down and thrown out of the hall.

Narcissistic-destructive communication

Instead of a constructive (self-)critical dialogue, one finds a pronounced narcissistic-destructive communication. The idea of thesis, antithesis and synthesis is a distant memory for narcissists. Out of fear of reality and change, narcissists use both attacks against the person of the "opponent" and rhetorical subtleties as a defense.

Such "discussions" can and should lead to nothing other than the confirmation of the narcissistic self-image. And this usually comes at the expense of the "discussion" partner, who is devalued as a person.

1.14   No meta-level

An interesting phenomenon in narcissists is the extensive inability to analyse - especially their own behaviour - on a meta-level. Critically examining one's own actions from a more objective, higher-level perspective and in interaction with the environment is, understandably, almost impossible. Narcissists are thus denied access to the insight that one cannot refute the accusation of narcissistic (destructive) behaviour by continuing the very behaviour that is being criticized. Instead, the critic is usually attacked as a person, as already mentioned. The extensive lack of reflection on a meta-level is another important building block for the "narcissism trap".

1.15   Summary

The first thing that comes to mind with narcissists is their overvaluation of their own person and their egocentrism. However, other aspects are much more central to understanding narcissism and the consequences that result from it. On the one hand, there is the separation from reality in order not to endanger one's own self-image.
The paths to rational solutions for the complex demands of life, let alone on a meta-level, are often blocked. Everything new and every change causes fear and defensiveness.

„Der Nervöse trägt das Gefühl der Unsicherheit ständig mit sich. Daher ist sein 'analogisches Denken', sind seine Lösungsversuche nach Analogie älterer Erfahrungen

stärker und deutlicher ausgeprägt. Sein Misoneismus (Lombroso) [Neophobie], seine Furcht vor dem Neuen, vor Entscheidungen und Prüfungen – die immer vorhanden sind -, stammen aus dem mangelnden Glauben an sich selbst. Er hat sich so sehr an Leitlinien gekettet, nimmt diese wörtlich und sucht sie zu realisieren, dass er, ohne es zu wissen, darauf verzichtet hat, unbefangen, ohne Vorurteil an die Lösung realer Fragen zu gehen." [Adler (1977)][17]

Instead of constructive (self-)critical communication, one is more likely to find narcissistic-destructive communication that attacks personally instead of trying to analyze and discuss the problems and possible solutions.
Added to this is the increased fear of change, combined with strong auto-/destructive impulses. The destructive

---

17 Nervous people carry a feeling of insecurity with them all the time. This is why their 'analogical thinking', their attempts to find solutions based on previous experiences, are stronger and more pronounced. Their misoneism (Lombroso) [neophobia], their fear of the new, of decisions and tests - which are always present - stem from a lack of belief in themselves. They have chained themselves so tightly to guidelines, taking them literally and trying to implement them, that they have, without knowing it, renounced the ability to approach the solution of real questions impartially and without prejudice.

actions satisfy the need for effectiveness. The auto-destructive actions arise as a reaction to an environment that is perceived as threatening, as an attempt to defend against a perceived enemy.

„Der Egoismus nervöser Menschen, ihr Neid, ihr Geiz, ihnen oft bewußt, ihre Tendenz, Menschen und Dinge zu entwerten, stammen aus ihrem Gefühl der Unsicherheit und sind bestimmt, sie zu sichern, zu lenken, anzuspornen, sich zu überheben. - Da sie in Phantasien eingesponnen sind und in der Zukunft leben, ist auch ihre Zerstreutheit nicht verwunderlich. - Der Stimmungswechsel ist abhängig vom Spiel ihrer Phantasie, die bald peinliche Erinnerungen berührt, bald sich aufschwingt zu Erwartung des Triumphes, analog dem Schwanken und Zweifeln des Neurotikers, dem besten Mittel, Entscheidungen auszuweichen. Dabei spielt ihre Empfindlichkeit so wie Pessimismus eine hervorragende Rolle."
[Adler (1977)][18]

---

18 The egoism of nervous people, their envy, their avarice, which they are often aware of, their tendency to devalue people and things, stem from their feeling of insecurity and are designed to protect them, to guide them, to encourage them, to elevate themselves. - Since they are wrapped up in fantasies and live in the future, their absent-mindedness is not surprising. - The change of mood depends on the play

3   Society

Let us now turn to society and the narcissistic structures within it. It is of course to be expected that similar things have already been described at least in part by other authors. We therefore want to look at previous approaches and analyze similarities as well as differences.

1.16   Previous approaches

3.1.a   Le Bon: mass psychology

On the one hand, Le Bon's mass psychology is the exact opposite of our approach. For Le Bon, the (rational) individual and the (irrational) mass are two clearly separate structures. For Le Bon, a qualitative change takes place when the individual becomes part of a mass. For us, however, the behavior of the individual, group, mass and society is a continuum with corresponding interactions.

---

of their imagination, which sometimes touches on painful memories, sometimes rises to the expectation of triumph, analogous to the wavering and doubting of the neurotic, the best way to avoid making decisions. Their sensitivity as well as pessimism play an outstanding role in this.

On the other hand, however, Le Bon describes precisely the characteristics of a group that, from our perspective, are symptoms of symbiotic narcissism as a group phenomenon.

„Massenpsychologie und Massengesellschaft: Die in der Masse aktivierten Gefühle, Ideen und Urteile zeichnen sich nach Le Bon durch folgende Merkmale aus: Massen reagieren triebhaft, sind **extrem erregbar und neigen zu spontanen, ungehemmten, affektgesteuerten und unmittelbaren Handlungen***. Massen befinden sich im Zustand gespannter Erwartung, sie sind deshalb leicht beeinflußbar und leichtgläubig. Einseitigkeit, Überschwänglichkeit und Suggestibilität bewahren die Massen vor Zweifel und Ungewißheit.* **Aus dem Dogmatismus und Konservativismus der Massen gegenüber Meinungen, Ideen und Glaubenssätzen resultieren ihre Unduldsamkeit und Herrschsucht gegenüber Andersdenkenden***. Massen entwickeln eine Vorliebe für bestimmte Personen (Idole), Lehrmeinungen und Grundideen. Sie können von Ideen aber nur dann stark beeinflußt werden, wenn diese ihnen nicht in abstrakter, sondern in bildhafter, symbolischer Form dargeboten werden. Dazu müssen die Ideen umgeformt und für die Massen aufbereitet werden, wobei nicht ihre Logik und Folgerichtigkeit, sondern ihre Einfachheit und Anschaulichkeit die Akzeptanzbereit-*

schaft bei der Masse bestimmt. **Die Logik der Massenur-
teile beruht nicht auf tatsächlich logischen, deduktiv
aufeinander folgenden Schlüssen**, *sondern auf der Verknüpfung von ähnlich erscheinenden Dingen und Ereig-
nissen, die nur eine oberflächliche Beziehung zueinander
haben sowie in der vorschnellen Verallgemeinerung von
Einzelfällen.* **Die Logik der Massen basiert somit auf
Analogieschlüssen**, *mit denen auch von der Sache her
Widersprüchliches oder Ungleiches miteinander verbunden werden kann. Die Einbildungskraft der Massen ist
durch einfache, klare und emotionsgeladene Bilder so
stark erregbar, daß diese Bilder und Symbole für die Realität selbst gehalten werden. Gerade das Einfache und
dabei Übertriebene und Sensationelle spricht die Massen
an und steuert ihr Denken und Verhalten.* **Die Bindung
der Massen an ein erhabenes Ziel und einen dieses Ziel
verkörpernden übermächtigen Führer zeigt nach Le
Bon ihren fundamentalen Bezug zu religiösen Elemen-
ten.** *Der Führer wird angebetet, verehrt und gefürchtet.
Es kommt zur blinden Unterwerfung unter seine Befehle.*
**Die von den Massen vertretenen Grundideen werden
nicht kritisch untersucht, sondern mit missionarischem
Eifer verbreitet und alle, die ihnen nicht folgen wollen,
werden als Feinde behandelt.**" [Thomas (1992)][19]

---

19 Mass psychology and mass society: According to Le Bon,
the feelings, ideas and judgements activated in the masses

What we have described as characteristic characteristics of narcissists, the irrationality and ideological affinity, the refusal to perceive reality, the destructive impulses..., Le Bon describes all of this as characteristics of masses. For Le Bon, "mass" is not simply a large gathering of people, such as at open-air concerts, who, for example,

---

are characterized by the following features: Masses react instinctively, are extremely excitable and tend to spontaneous, uninhibited, emotionally driven and immediate actions. Masses are in a state of tense expectation, they are therefore easily influenced and gullible. One-sidedness, exuberance and suggestibility protect the masses from doubt and uncertainty. The dogmatism and conservatism of the masses towards opinions, ideas and beliefs result in their intolerance and desire to dominate those who think differently. Masses develop a preference for certain people (idols), doctrines and basic ideas. However, they can only be strongly influenced by ideas if they are presented to them in a pictorial, symbolic form rather than in an abstract form. To do this, the ideas must be transformed and prepared for the masses, whereby the willingness of the masses to accept them is determined not by their logic and consistency, but by their simplicity and clarity. The logic of mass judgments is not based on actually logical, deductively consecutive conclusions, but on the linking of seemingly similar things and events that only have a superficial relationship to one another, as well as on the hasty generalizati-

instinctively behave like a herd when panicking.

What Le Bon describes as "mass" in the field of social psychology is a large group that does not require any physical connection.

What is today understood by the findings of social psychology and sociology of knowledge as being mediated by participation in groups and "communities of practice" [Wenger (1998)], Le Bon still considers to be an inherited "racial soul".

„Unsere bewussten Akte leiten sich aus einem, besonders durch Vererbungseinflüsse geschaffenen, unbe-

---

on of individual cases. The logic of the masses is therefore based on analogical conclusions, which can also connect contradictory or dissimilar things. The imagination of the masses is so strongly stimulated by simple, clear and emotionally charged images that these images and symbols are taken for reality itself. It is precisely the simple, yet exaggerated and sensational that appeals to the masses and controls their thinking and behavior. According to Le Bon, the masses' attachment to a lofty goal and an overpowering leader who embodies this goal shows its fundamental connection to religious elements. The leader is worshipped, revered and feared. Blind submission to his orders ensues. The basic ideas represented by the masses are not critically examined, but are spread with missionary zeal and all those who do not want to follow them are treated as enemies.

*wussten **Substrat** her. Dieses enthält die zahllosen Ahnenspuren, aus denen sich die Rassenseele konstituiert. Hinter den eingestandenen Motiven unserer Handlungen gibt es zweifellos die geheimen Gründe, die wir nicht eingestehen, hinter diesen aber liegen noch geheimere, die wir nicht einmal kennen. Die Mehrzahl unserer alltäglichen Handlungen ist nur die Wirkung verborgener, uns entgehender Motive.*

*Es sind vornehmlich die der Rassenseele zugrunde liegenden **unbewussten Elemente**, wodurch sich alle Individuen dieser Rasse ähneln; und sie, die Produkte der Erziehung, noch mehr aber einer außerordentlichen Erblichkeit, sind es auch, wodurch sie sich unterscheiden. Die an Intelligenz unähnlichsten Menschen haben äußerst ähnliche Triebe, Leidenschaften und Gefühle. In allem, was Gegenstand des Gefühls ist: Religion, Politik, Moral, Sympathien und Antipathien usw. überragen die ausgezeichnetsten Menschen nur sehr selten das Niveau der gewöhnlichsten Individuen. Zwischen einem großen Mathematiker und seinem Schuster kann intellektuell ein Abgrund klaffen, aber hinsichtlich des Charakters ist der Unterschied sehr oft nichtig oder sehr gering."*
[Le Bon (1895/2016)][20]

---

20 Our conscious acts are derived from an unconscious substrate, created primarily by hereditary influences. This contains the countless ancestral traces from which the racial

Le Bon describes the unconscious aspects and foundations of behavior very well, but attributes these to inheritance within a race. From today's perspective, including cross-cultural social psychology, it is the transmission of characteristics, values and behaviors of a culture through participation in it. The cultures differ quite significantly in this respect, as the following, actually intended to be funny, illustration shows:

---

soul is constituted. Behind the admitted motives of our actions there are undoubtedly secret reasons which we do not admit, but behind these lie even more secret ones which we do not even know. The majority of our everyday actions are only the effect of hidden motives which escape us.

It is primarily the unconscious elements underlying the racial soul that make all individuals of this race similar; and they, the products of education and even more of an extraordinary heredity, are also what makes them different. People who are the most dissimilar in intelligence have extremely similar drives, passions and feelings. In everything that is the subject of feeling: religion, politics, morality, sympathies and antipathies, etc., the most outstanding people only very rarely rise above the level of the most ordinary individuals. There may be an intellectual gulf between a great mathematician and his cobbler, but as far as character is concerned the difference is very often negligible or very small.

„Heaven is where the British are the policemen, the
French are the cooks, the Germans are the mechanics,
the Italians are the lovers and everything is organized by
the Swiss.
Hell is where the British are the cooks, the French are the
mechanics, the Swiss are the lovers, the Germans are the
policemen and everything is organized by the Italians."
[Source: unknown]

3.1.b   Fromm: Group Narcissism

Erich Fromm gives the following description of "group
narcissism":

„Wenn, wie beim Gruppennarzißmus, das Objekt nicht
der einzelne, sondern die Gruppe ist, der er angehört,
kann sich der einzelne dieses Narzißmus voll bewußt sein
und ihn ohne Hemmungen zum Ausdruck bringen. Die
Behauptung, daß »mein Vaterland« (oder meine Nation
oder meine Religion) am wunderbarsten, kultiviertesten,
mächtigsten, friedliebendsten usw. ist, klingt durchaus
nicht verrückt. Im Gegenteil, es klingt nach Patriotismus,
Glaube und Loyalität. Außerdem erscheint es als ein rea-
listisches und vernünftiges Werturteil, da es von vielen
Mitgliedern der gleichen Gruppe geteilt wird. Dieser
Konsensus bringt es fertig, die Phantasie in eine Realität

umzuwandeln, **da Realität für die meisten Menschen
durch den allgemeinen Konsensus erzeugt wird und
sich nicht auf vernünftige oder kritische Überlegungen
gründet.** *Der Gruppennarzißmus hat wichtige Funktio-
nen.* **Vor allem fördert er die Solidarität und den inne-
ren Zusammenhalt der Gruppe und erleichtert ihre
Manipulation, da er an narzißtische Vorurteile appel-
liert.** *Zweitens ist er außerordentlich wichtig als ein Element, das den Mitgliedern der Gruppe Befriedigung ver-
schafft, vor allem jenen unter ihnen, die an sich wenig
Grund hätten, sich stolz und schätzenswert zu finden.
Wenn man das armseligste, ärmste und am wenigsten
respektierte Mitglied einer Gruppe ist, wird man für
seinen elenden Zustand durch das Gefühl entschädigt:
»Ich bin ein Teil der wundervollsten Gruppe der Welt.
Ich, der ich in Wirklichkeit ein armseliger Wurm bin,
werde zum Riesen dadurch, daß ich zu dieser Gruppe
gehöre.«* **Folglich entspricht der Grad des Gruppennarzißmus dem Mangel an wirklicher Befriedigung im
Leben.** *Jene sozialen Klassen, die ihr Leben mehr genie-
ßen, sind weniger fanatisch (Fanatismus ist eine charak-
teristische Eigenschaft des Gruppennarzißmus) als die,
welche wie das Kleinbürgertum an einem Mangel auf
allen materiellen und kulturellen Gebieten leiden und ein*

75

Leben führen, das unerträglich langweilig ist.“
[Fromm (1989)][21]

Although Fromm sees the elevation of one's own self, he largely overlooks the other narcissistic characteristics we have described. And the idea that group narcissism is

---

21 When, as in group narcissism, the object is not the individual but the group to which he belongs, the individual can be fully aware of this narcissism and express it without inhibition. The assertion that "my country" (or my nation or my religion) is the most wonderful, most cultured, most powerful, most peace-loving, etc. does not sound at all crazy. On the contrary, it sounds like patriotism, faith and loyalty. Moreover, it appears to be a realistic and reasonable value judgment, since it is shared by many members of the same group. This consensus manages to transform fantasy into reality, since reality for most people is created by the general consensus and is not based on rational or critical considerations. Group narcissism has important functions. Above all, it promotes solidarity and internal cohesion within the group and facilitates its manipulation, since it appeals to narcissistic prejudices. Secondly, it is extremely important as an element which gives satisfaction to the members of the group, especially to those among them who in themselves would have little reason to feel proud and worthy of appreciation. If one is the most miserable, poorest and least respected member of a group, one is com-

caused by lack and boredom does not agree with our approach.

Fromm also only sees a relationship within the group in which an individual enhances his or her self-esteem through participation in a group. The mutual enhancement as symbiotic narcissism is not fully recognized.

3.1.c   Excursus: Symmetrical and Asymmetrical Relationship

To understand symbiotic narcissism as a group phenomenon, it is necessary to distinguish between a symmetrical (on an equal footing) and an asymmetrical (with a power imbalance) relationship. In an asymmetrical relationship, there is the alcoholic, narcissist... and the "matching" co-alcoholic, co-narcissist...

---

pensated for one's miserable condition by the feeling: "I am part of the most wonderful group in the world. I, who am really a miserable worm, become a giant by belonging to this group." Thus, the degree of group narcissism corresponds to the lack of real satisfaction in life. Those social classes which enjoy their lives more are less fanatical (fanaticism is a characteristic feature of group narcissism) than those which, like the petty bourgeoisie, suffer from deprivation in all material and cultural areas and lead a life which is unbearably dull.

A good example here is Sancho Panza, who, as the stable master of his master Don Quixote, is not subject to the distortion of reality that is usual for narcissists and also points out to his master the difference between his imagination and reality. But Sancho Panza stays with his master anyway because the latter has offered him the prospect of a governorship.

The "fight against windmills" is also, by the way, a typical sign of narcissists.

In a symmetrical relationship, there are no dependencies due to a power imbalance, but rather because the other person is mutually used to satisfy narcissistic needs. So it is the symbiotic connection of two or more narcissists, alcoholics...

In symbiotic narcissism, a symmetrical relationship means that everyone feels superior to everyone else involved. In the spirit of the saying:

„Nothing in the world is distributed as fairly as intelligence. Everyone thinks they have enough of it."
(René Descartes)

And one must probably add:
„... and more than anyone else."

Fromm therefore mainly sees individuals who satisfy their narcissism through belonging to a group that is not necessarily narcissistic. The strongly destructive tendencies are also largely overlooked. This constellation also exists, of course, but our focus is on the symmetrical symbiotic narcissism structures.

3.1.d   Authoritarian personality

With the construct of the "authoritarian personality" we are coming very close to symbiotic narcissism as a group phenomenon. And we will show that the authoritarian personality is a special (political) manifestation of symbiotic narcissism. This also makes the usefulness of both clinical social psychology and the construct of "symbiotic narcissism" clear. The use of the construct "authoritarian personality" to date has been very diverse.

„Since then, the history of the term has been characterized by the competition between different explanatory approaches:
• From a psychoanalytic point of view, the authoritarian character develops when the child's aggressive, instinctual and other needs are suppressed too strongly by parental demands for obedience and are ultimately directed at other people, socially weaker people or minorities;

• From a sociological point of view, the pressure to conform to repressive social conditions and hierarchical structures is primarily blamed;
• From a social psychological point of view, the thought patterns adopted from the family and other social reference groups are highlighted, i.e. attitudes and prejudices due to a lack of or incorrect knowledge about other groups of people;
• From a developmental psychology perspective, authority conflicts in a failed separation from the parents result in insufficient identity formation and independence, so that an authoritarian structured dependency persists;
• From the perspective of differential psychology, the interaction of a behavioral disposition and a "suitable" trigger situation is important in order to make it clear that authoritarian behavior does not manifest itself uniformly, but depends on the individual disposition and the respective situation." [Source: de.wikipedia.org]

Here we follow a representation of the "authoritarian personality" from a social psychological perspective:

„Darüber hinaus führt die Enge des eigenen Horizonts als Folge der Verdrängung zum mangelnden Verständnis für andere Gruppen, seien es Nationen oder Sub-Kulturen des eigenen Volkes. Die Projektion eigener abgelehn-

ter Impulse nach außen wird weiter dazu beitragen, daß das Unverständnis für andere zu einer Abwertung des Fremden wird, verbunden mit einer Aufwertung der eigenen Lebensart. Das führt einmal zum Nationalismus und zum anderen zum Vorurteil. Solche Menschen werden Einwanderungsbeschränkungen für bestimmte Gruppen befürworten, sie werden Gastarbeiter, Asylanten und Ausländer überhaupt vom sozialen Leben abzusondern suchen. Da sie in der Fremdgruppe eigene abgelehnte Tendenzen wiederzuerkennen glauben, werden sie aktiv nach Fremdkörpern in der Gesellschaft suchen und sie diskriminieren. Nur wenn diese anderen Gruppen ganz eindeutig stärker sind, wird man sich ihnen unterwerfen. *Eine der zentralen Tendenzen, die von der autoritären Persönlichkeit in anderen Menschen bekämpft wird, ist die eigene Schwäche.* Diese projizierte Furcht vor der eigenen Schwäche verhindert die Entwicklung von Mitleid für die Schwachen. Sie argumentieren also wahrscheinlich gegen Wohlfahrtsmaßnahmen, Gefangenenfürsorge, Ausländerintegration und für die Anwendung der Todesstrafe. *Da die autoritäre Persönlichkeit innerlich unsicher ist und fortwährend der Bestätigung von außen durch Gruppenmaßstäbe bedarf, ist sie ständig gezwungen, die eigene Gruppe zu verteidigen, denn für sie bedeutet ein Angriff auf die Gruppe auch einen Angriff auf das eigene Selbst.* Das führt innenpolitisch zu einer **Intoleranz**

81

denen gegenüber, die von den Gruppenmaßstäben abwei-
chen wollen. Außenpolitisch ist eine mögliche Konse-
quenz dieser Unsicherheit und der Projektion abgelehn-
ter Tendenzen das Gefühl der Bedrohung. So ein Mensch
ist schon aus diesem Grund fremdenfeindlich. Er sieht
das eigene Land ständig der Gefahr der Einkreisung und
der Bedrohung von außen ausgesetzt. Die einzige Ant-
wort auf dieses Gefühl ist sein Verlangen nach mehr
Macht für das eigene Land, denn im Denken des autoritä-
*ren Menschen **begegnet man einer Bedrohung nur da-***
durch, daß man selber stärker und rücksichtsloser ist
***als die anderen.**"* [Thomas (1992)][22]

---

22 Furthermore, the narrowness of one's own horizon as a
    result of repression leads to a lack of understanding for
    other groups, be they nations or sub-cultures of one's own
    people. The projection of one's own rejected impulses out-
    wards will further contribute to the fact that the lack of
    understanding for others turns into a devaluation of the fo-
    reign, combined with an appreciation of one's own way of
    life. This leads to nationalism on the one hand and to preju-
    dice on the other. Such people will support immigration
    restrictions for certain groups, they will try to isolate guest
    workers, asylum seekers and foreigners from social life in
    general. Because they believe they recognize their own
    rejected tendencies in the foreign group, they will actively
    look for foreign bodies in society and discriminate against
    them. Only if these other groups are clearly stronger will

On the one hand, the components of narcissistic personalities that we have described, intolerance and destructiveness, become clear. It is also indirectly stated that people with authoritarian personalities need a group, a state... to which they feel they belong and which they must defend. What is not seen, however, is the absolutely necessary

---

people submit to them. One of the central tendencies that the authoritarian personality fights in other people is their own weakness. This projected fear of one's own weakness prevents the development of compassion for the weak. So they probably argue against welfare measures, prisoner care, integration of foreigners and for the use of the death penalty. Since the authoritarian personality is internally insecure and constantly needs external confirmation through group standards, he is constantly forced to defend his own group, because for him an attack on the group also means an attack on himself. In domestic politics this leads to intolerance towards those who want to deviate from group standards. In foreign politics one possible consequence of this insecurity and the projection of rejected tendencies is the feeling of being threatened. Such a person is xenophobic for this reason alone. He sees his own country constantly at risk of encirclement and threat from outside. The only answer to this feeling is his desire for more power for his own country, because in the mind of the authoritarian person one can only counter a threat by being stronger and more ruthless than the others.

gathering of several individuals with authoritarian personalities who confirm each other. Confirmation by an
anonymous group will not be enough to protect oneself.
The authoritarian personality is also primarily associated
with the right-wing political spectrum.

The approach of symbiotic narcissism as a group phenomenon, however, makes it clear that an authoritarian
personality is a specific manifestation that has all of the
characteristics mentioned.

And the criticism of the construct can also be resolved.

„*It has often been criticized that insufficient distinction is
made between the authoritarian personality and ordinary
conservatism. In addition, authoritarianism exists not only at the right but also at the left extreme of political attitudes - as Hans Jürgen Eysenck and Milton Rokeach
have shown. Edward Shils objected that the study was
based on an outdated political right-left division.*"
[Source: wikipedia.org]

In the chapter "antagonistic symbiotic narcissism" we
will explain that the need for boundaries and enemies in
order to maintain psychological balance can lead to antagonistic structures in which symbiotic narcissistic
groups on both sides fight each other without running the
risk of actually changing anything. The antagonism

between left-wing radicals and right-wing radicals, who give each other a right to exist and a purpose, is an example here.

4   Symbiotic Narcissism

Symbiotic narcissism is a group phenomenon, whereby two people can also form a group.

The individual/dyadic perspectives used so far are not sufficient to understand symbiotic relationships. The interactions within the group must be considered.
• Narcissistic relationships occur in groups in both of the forms already described, symbiotic, i.e. symmetrical on the same
level
• in an asymmetrical relationship between narcissist(s) and co-narcissist

The communication and interaction of these groups with the environment is parallel to that of narcissistic individuals, as we have already described.
Symbiotic narcissism will not occur in its pure form in groups. In groups, there are usually both destructive symbiotic-narcissistic and constructive components. It is therefore primarily a question of the relationship between

these components. But it should not be surprising that in a society described as narcissistic, there are many groups that primarily have symbiotic-narcissistic elements and satisfy corresponding needs.

The common tenor of these groups is the now widespread "against", which on the one hand satisfies the (destructive) need for effectiveness, but without entailing the danger of change. Constructive approaches are lacking in groups in which symbiotic-narcissistic structures predominate. For these groups, the general rule is that the more spectacular and senseless an action - the better.

Rationally speaking, the actions of Greenpeace, for example, do not entail the danger of (positive) change. You can climb up chimneys as often as you like, chain yourself to something, cruise ships in front of whaling fleets... but that will probably and almost certainly change little. The main effect of such actions is that they satisfy the narcissism of the participants and members.

By distinguishing between narcissistic destructiveness (against) and constructive-(self-)critical action, one can differentiate very well between groups and the symbiotic-narcissistic structures present in them.

1.17 Animal and environmental protection

In the area of animal and environmental protection, for example, the proportion of symbiotic-narcissistic structures is comparatively low in animal welfare associations, which in principle have an actively positive effect.
But there are also groups and associations in which the narcissistic-destructive component far outweighs the others. At this point we would like to remind you of Socrates' saying. Organizations that focus on "against" are guaranteed a large audience because this is the basis for satisfying narcissistic needs.

„Man wird viel leichter durch Zorn, Wut, Grausamkeit oder die Leidenschaft zu zerstören erregt als durch Liebe und produktives und aktives Interesse.
*Die erste Art der Erregung erfordert nicht, daß der Betreffende sich anstrengt - **denn man braucht keine Geduld und keine Disziplin dazu, man braucht nichts zu lernen, man muß sich nicht konzentrieren, man muß auf nichts verzichten, und man braucht nicht kritisch zu denken, braucht seinen Narzißmus und seine Gier nicht zu überwinden.** Für den der in seinem seelischen Wachstum zurückgeblieben ist, sind »einfache Reize« immer zur Hand, oder er kann sie leicht produzieren.*

*Über Stimuli wie Unfälle, Feuersbrünste, Verbrechen
oder Kriege kann man in der Zeitung lesen, man kann
von ihnen im Rundfunk hören, oder man kann sie sich im
Fernsehen oder im Kino ansehen. Auch kann man sie
selbst produzieren, **indem man sich einen Grund sucht
zu hassen, zu zerstören und andere zu beherrschen.**
(Wie stark dieses Bedürfnis ist, zeigt sich an den Millio-
nen von Dollars, die die Massenmedien damit verdienen,
daß sie diese Art der Erregung verkaufen.)*"
[Fromm (1989)][23]

---

23   One is much more easily aroused by anger, rage, cruelty, or
     the passion to destroy than by love and productive and
     active interest. The first kind of arousal does not require
     any effort on the part of the person concerned - for it requi-
     res no patience or discipline, no learning, no concentration,
     no sacrifice, no critical thinking, no overcoming narcissism
     and greed. For the person who is psychically retarded,
     "simple stimuli" are always at hand, or can be easily pro-
     duced. Stimuli such as accidents, fires, crimes, or wars can
     be read about in the newspaper, heard about on the radio,
     or seen on television or in the movies. They can also be
     produced by oneself by looking for a reason to hate, de-
     stroy, and dominate others. (The strength of this need is
     shown by the millions of dollars that the mass media earn
     by selling this kind of arousal.)

By being "against" it, especially in a collective form, both contact with the sometimes stubborn reality that contradicts one's own self-image and the fear of change are avoided!

1.18   Science

Symbiotic-narcissistic structures can also be found in many parts of science (unfortunately). Science is defined in a circular argument as what the "scientific community" does. And the "scientific community" includes anyone who does science. So you go around in circles like a cat chasing its own tail. The symbiotic-narcissistic dimension is realized by distancing yourself from the outside world. Contrary to the scientific principle that a statement must be checked independently of the speaker, only statements within the "scientific community" are accepted.
A constructive (self-)critical discourse, both within and beyond the boundaries of the "community", is hardly possible, On the one hand, this results in massive distortions of perception, as described by David Dunning.

„On average, people tend to hold overly favorable views of themselves. They overestimate their skill, their knowledge, their moral character, and theri place on the social ladder. Ironically, they even overestimate their ability to

*provide veridical and unbiased judgments about themsel-
ves. ... Indeed, such overly rosy views of self can be
found among the population I could describe as the
wisest, most learned, and contemplative in modern society. Namely, 94% of college professors say they do above
average work ... In a similar vein, academic researchers
think their manuscripts that they submit for publication
possess more methodological and theoretical value than
the manuscripts of others."* [Dunning (2012)]

In our opinion, it is the lack of constructive (self-)critical
discourse within science that leads to such results.
What is more threatening to society, however, is that science has also lost its orientation due to this lack.
In his book "Systematicity" [Hoyningen-Huene (2013)],
the philosopher of science Hoyningen-Huene attempts to
characterize the difference between science and common
knowledge by membership of the "scientific community"
on the one hand, and "systematicity" as a particularly
systematic approach on the other.
In doing so, he overlooks three points:
• the circular definition of the "scientific community",
• the violation of the basic scientific rule of speaker independence caused by the condition of membership,

• and the fact that mistakes that are made systematically do not become knowledge.

On the other hand, a constructive (self-)critical dialogue as the basis of science is not to be found.
However, Hoyningen-Huene is (unfortunately) not alone in this. The philosophy of science currently hardly goes beyond the postulation of a "scientific community" as the basis of science. And due to a lack of knowledge of social psychology, it is overlooked that all "communities", whether "scientific" or not, show one thing above all: unconscious, irrational group behavior. The "scientific community" is therefore not constitutive of science - on the contrary, it is its biggest problem! And so, from a social psychological perspective, it is not surprising that in the field of autism research, tens of thousands of scientists have collectively gone in the wrong direction or gone around in circles for more than 50 years [Schmidt (2017)].

1.19   Esotericism

The very rapid rise of esoteric movements and schools is above all an expression of a deep irrationality.
Esoteric practices and theories are always based on a Manichaean view of separation, with a "dirty" body as a prison on the one hand, and a divine soul as a prisoner of

the body on the other. At the same time, esotericism serves as an escape from reality and satisfies the need for effectiveness on the other. And this is also very strong in a supposedly heroic fight against external enemies such as gluten, lactose, intestinal bacteria, aging, ...

We must leave it to later discussions to discuss the question of when - not only in the esoteric scene - Manichaeism ends and narcissism begins.

Or whether Manichaeism is perhaps a specific form of narcissism?

The narcissistic components in the area of esotericism are the enhancement of one's own self by overestimating one's own abilities. Everyone thinks they are healers and fights against supposed evil through diets, self-awareness courses, yoga...

The reality with all its frustrating and frightening phenomena is ignored. Instead, everything is explained using astrology, biographical work, reincarnation, homeopathy, etc. and not only treatable but curable through appropriate "therapies".

You just have to find the right globules, then all the misery in this world can be cured. Everything appears to be able to be influenced positively, e.g. through "healing rituals" and "giving energy", and this can also be done via email.

Just as Nordic walkers keep nature at bay with their walking sticks, so do esotericists with their rituals.

If the esoteric movement continues to grow at the same rate, a point will soon be reached where there will only be healers and no more sick people.

It is important to note that esotericism only functions as symbiotic narcissism, i.e. as a group in which people support and affirm each other. And together they create an irrational parallel world. Reality in its current form is largely and above all mutually ignored. Instead, people turn to a dreamed-of ideal past of seers and shamans and a perfect future.

5   Antagonistic symbiotic narcissism

Our thesis is that wherever a symbiotic narcissistic group forms, an antagonistic one will often form as well.

In the section on the authoritarian personality, we already addressed the antagonism between the extreme left and right. So far, only the elements of the elevation of the in-group and the devaluation of the out-group have been described in this context.

„Diejenigen, deren Narziβmus mehr ihre Gruppe als sie selbst betrifft, sind ebenso empfindlich wie individuelle

93

Narzißten, und **sie reagieren wütend auf jede wirkliche oder eingebildete Beleidigung, die ihrer Gruppe angetan wird.** *Sie reagieren womöglich nur noch intensiver und ganz gewiß bewußter darauf. Ein einzelner wird, wenn er nicht gerade geisteskrank ist, wenigstens manchmal einige Zweifel in Bezug auf sein narzißtisches Selbst-Image hegen. Das Mitglied einer Gruppe kennt solche Zweifel nicht, da die Mehrheit seinen Narzißmus teilt.* **Im Falle eines Konfliktes zwischen verschiedenen Gruppen, die ihren kollektiven Narzißmus gegenseitig herausfordern, ruft diese Herausforderung eine intensive wechselseitige Feindschaft hervor.** *Das narzißtische Image der eigenen Gruppe wird aufs höchste gesteigert, während man die feindliche Gruppe möglichst herabsetzt. Die eigene Gruppe wird zum Verteidiger der menschlichen Würde, des Anstandes, der Moral und des Rechts. Die andere Gruppe wird verteufelt. Sie ist betrügerisch, skrupellos, grausam und von Grund auf unmenschlich. Die Beleidigung eines Symbols des Gruppennarzißmus – zum Beispiel der Fahne oder der Person des Kaisers, des Präsidenten oder eines Gesandten – ruft als Reaktion beim Volk eine so intensive Wut und Aggression hervor, daß es sogar bereit ist, seine Führer in ihrer Kriegspolitik zu unterstützen."* [Fromm (1989)] [24]

---

24 Those whose narcissism concerns their group rather than themselves are as sensitive as individual narcissists, and

However, an appreciation of the in-group and a devaluation of out-groups is necessary but not sufficient for the diagnosis of an underlying narcissistic structure.

The "minimal group paradigm" by Tajfel shows what minimal prerequisites are sufficient to create an unconscious group membership and the resulting preference for the in-group.

In contrast, the points we mentioned are essential for

---

they react angrily to any real or imagined insult to their group. They may only react more intensely and certainly more consciously. An individual, unless he is insane, will at least sometimes have some doubts about his narcissistic self-image. The member of a group has no such doubts, since the majority shares his narcissism. In the case of a conflict between different groups challenging each other's collective narcissism, the challenge produces intense mutual hostility. The narcissistic image of one's own group is heightened to the highest degree, while the enemy group is belittled as much as possible. One's own group becomes the defender of human dignity, decency, morality and justice. The other group is demonized as deceitful, unscrupulous, cruel and fundamentally inhuman. The insult of a symbol of group narcissism - for example, the flag or the person of the emperor, the president, or an envoy - provokes in the people a reaction so intense anger and aggression that they are even prepared to support their leaders in their war policy.

identifying a symbiotic-narcissistic group structure, such as:

1. Denial or ignorance of reality
2. Anxiety of change
3. Rigid ideologies
4. No constructive (self-)critical communication
5. Satisfying the need for effectiveness through destructiveness
6. Ignoring differences in competence
7. …

From this perspective, it becomes clear how similar the extreme right and left are. Both sides supposedly strive for a perfect world, but are incapable of constructive (self-)critical action.

And they give each other a right to exist through the "fight against the political opponent".

What would extremist demonstrations be without a counter-demonstration from the other side?

In this way, two groups that are narcissistic in their basic structure form a very stable antagonistic symbiotic system. They give each other a right to exist and a task at the same time.

„Allerdings liegen einige klassische Symptome offen zutage; die eindeutig auf die Wirksamkeit des erläuterten Projektionsmechanismus schließen lassen: Dazu gehören unter anderem **projektive Wahrnehmungseinengungen und -Verzerrungen: Man sieht Aggression, Imperialismus, Menschenrechtsverletzungen nur auf der einen Seite der Welt.** *Fernerhin gehört dazu eine Bereitschaft zu einer generalisierenden Entwertung: Man bezieht die im kommunistischen Machtbereich lebenden Völker in allgemeine Klischeevorstellungen von Unkultiviertheit, Primitivität, Aggressivität ein. Auf der gleichen Linie liegt die ins Paranoide gesteigerte Befürchtung, im eigenen Lager vom Feinde unterwandert, verführt, angesteckt und verdorben zu werden: Wo sich im eigenen Kreis Kritik meldet, wo Arbeiter und Gewerkschaften unbequeme Forderungen steilen, wo die Frauen gegen Sexismus, die Studenten gegen Hochschulmißstände, die Schüler gegen Mängel des Schulwesens, wo die Bürgerinitiativen gegen Kernkraftwerke protestieren, wittern viele sogleich stereotyp östliche Fernsteuerung.“* [Richter (1982)]²⁵

---

25 However, some classic symptoms are evident, which clearly indicate the effectiveness of the projection mechanism described above. These include, among other things, projective narrowing and distortion of perception: aggression, imperialism, and human rights violations are only seen on one side of the world. Furthermore, it involves a willing-

The "projective perception limitations and distortions" are found in all symbiotic narcissistic groups due to the need to ignore reality. An antagonistic structure such as the opposition between communism and capitalism, i.e. formerly West and East, has a stabilizing effect on both sides. The difference between these is irrelevant, as the following old joke shows:

„What is the difference between communism and capitalism?

In capitalism, people exploit people…in communism, it is the other way around.“

---

ness to generalize: people living in the communist sphere of influence are included in general clichés of unculturedness, primitiveness, and aggressiveness. Along the same lines is the fear, which is heightened to the point of paranoia, of being infiltrated, seduced, infected, and corrupted by the enemy in one's own camp: when criticism is raised within one's own circle, when workers and unions make uncomfortable demands, when women protest against sexism, students against university abuses, schoolchildren against deficiencies in the school system, when citizens' initiatives protest against nuclear power plants, many immediately suspect stereotypical Eastern remote control.

6   Causes?

After we have identified "symbiotic narcissism as a group phenomenon" as a defining feature of our era and presented the distinguishing features, the question of the causes remains.

In the Victorian era, it was primarily the tightness, not only of corsets but also of moral concepts, that led to powerlessness as a hysterical symptom, what are then the conditions for the appearance of narcissism in this social form and intensity? In the following, we will attempt to provide some answers - without claiming to be complete.

1.20   Loss of touch with reality?

At the beginning of the book, the quote from Lowen described the unreality that accompanies both narcissistic personalities and societies.

But unreality works in both directions, can be cause and effect. And so our question is whether it is not the loss of connection to reality, caused by technical and social development, that contributes to the emergence of narcissism.

But what is meant by loss of connection to reality? In the past, people who, for example, brought the most meat back from the hunt as hunters were respected.

Today, when a trip to the nearest supermarket is enough to buy a vacuum-packed piece of meat, people who write the most beautiful novels about hunting are respected. People's actions and omissions no longer receive direct feedback from nature or "Not-wendigkeiten" (necessities). Thanks to technical and logistical progress, people's actions are no longer characterized by necessity, but by arbitrariness.

„Wir müssen hier noch einmal auf einen der grundlegendsten Begriffe Freuds zurückkommen, nämlich das »Realitätsprinzip«, das sich auf den Selbsterhaltungstrieb gründet, gegenüber dem »Lustprinzip«, das auf dem Sexualtrieb basiert. Ob wir vom Sexualtrieb oder von einer nicht-sexuellen Leidenschaft, in der ein bestimmter Charakterzug verwurzelt ist, getrieben werden, immer bleibt der Konflikt zwischen dem, was wir tun möchten, und den Anforderungen unseres Selbstinteresses von ausschlaggebender Bedeutung. Wir können uns nicht immer so verhalten, wie es uns unsere Leidenschaften eingeben, da wir unser Verhalten bis zu einem gewissen Grade modifizieren müssen, um am Leben zu bleiben.
Der Durchschnittsmensch bemüht sich um einen Kompromiß zwischen dem, was er seinem Charakter entsprechend gerne tun möchte, und dem, was er tun muß, um

nicht mehr oder weniger peinliche Konsequenzen auf sich nehmen zu müssen." [Fromm (1989)][26]

In a technologically affluent society, also characterized by almost limitless voyeurism and exhibitionism, the "reality principle" has largely been lost. Information is often no longer necessary for survival; it no longer creates a connection to reality, but rather separates people from it.

"Wie Thoreau angedeutet hatte, machte die Telegraphie die Relevanz irrelevant. Der Überfluß an Informationen hatte mit denen, an die er sich richtete, mit einem sozia-

---

26 We must return here to one of Freud's most fundamental concepts, namely the "reality principle" based on the instinct of self-preservation, as opposed to the "pleasure principle" based on the sexual instinct. Whether we are driven by the sexual instinct or by a non-sexual passion in which a particular character trait is rooted, the conflict between what we want to do and the demands of our self-interest remains of crucial importance. We cannot always behave as our passions dictate, since we must modify our behavior to a certain extent in order to stay alive. The average person strives to find a compromise between what he would like to do according to his character and what he must do in order to avoid more or less embarrassing consequences.

*len oder intellektuellen Kontext, in den ihr Leben einge-
bettet war, nichts oder nur wenig zu tun. ...*

*Doch der größte Teil der täglichen Nachrichten bleibt
wirkungslos, besteht aus Informationen, über die wir
reden können, die uns jedoch nicht zu sinnvollem Handeln veranlassen. Dies ist das wichtigste Vermächtnis des
Telegraphen: Dadurch, daß er eine Fülle irrelevanter
Informationen hervorbrachte, hat er das proportionale
Verhältnis zwischen Information und Aktion drastisch
verändert."* [Postman (1994)][27]

What was already clear with the invention and spread of
the telegraph is even more true today for television as a
"life surrogate extract". People no longer act in a real
world, but rather watch this world from a distance from
the "easy chair", the comfortable TV armchair.

---

27 As Thoreau suggested, the telegraph made relevance irrelevant. The abundance of information had little or nothing to
do with those to whom it was addressed, with any social or
intellectual context in which their lives were embedded. ...
But most of the daily news remains ineffective, consisting
of information that we can talk about but that does not lead
us to meaningful action. This is the most important legacy
of the telegraph: by producing a wealth of irrelevant information, it drastically changed the proportional relationship
between information and action.

„Der Pseudo-Kontext ist eine Struktur, die erfunden wird, um bruchstückhaften, belanglosen Informationen einen Scheinnutzen zuzuordnen.

Aber die Nutzanwendung, die sich aus dem Pseudo-Kontext ergibt, zielt nicht auf Handeln, auf das Lösen von Problemen oder auf Veränderung. Sie zielt auf das einzige, was man mit Informationen ohne wirkliche Beziehung zu unserem Dasein tun kann – sich amüsieren.

Der Pseudo-Kontext ist gleichsam die letzte Zuflucht einer von Belanglosigkeit, Inkohärenz und Ohnmacht überwältigten Kultur.“ [Postman (1994)][28]

Without feedback from reality, there is a lack of both orientation and correction of actions.

Action is no longer directed towards coping with necessities, but rather towards the fashions of the respective group of which one would like to be a member.

---

28 Pseudo-context is a structure invented to assign a pseudo-usefulness to fragmentary, irrelevant information. But the use that emerges from pseudo-context is not aimed at action, problem-solving, or change. It is aimed at the only thing that can be done with information that has no real connection to our existence - having fun. Pseudo-context is the last refuge of a culture overwhelmed by irrelevance, incoherence, and powerlessness.

1.21 Change of group structures?

Where does the postulated increase in narcissistic personalities come from?
Were clear group structures, such as those that existed a
few decades ago, perhaps a kind of protection?
Group structures that were defined, for example, by traditional costumes and dialects that have lasted for generations, gave people a clear orientation for centuries.
In the pursuit of freedom and individualism, people have
not abolished the need for group membership and unconscious group behavior.
But the clear structures that defined membership have be-
en lost.

*„Der Mensch braucht ein soziales System, in dem er sei-
nen Platz hat und in dem seine Beziehungen zu anderen
relativ stabil und durch allgemein anerkannte Werte und
Ideen gestützt sind. Was sich in der modernen Industrie-
gesellschaft ereignet hat, ist, daß die Traditionen, die
gemeinsamen Wertbegriffe und echten sozialen Bindungen weitgehend geschwunden sind.
Der moderne Massenmensch ist isoliert und einsam,
selbst dann, wenn er Teil einer Masse ist; er besitzt keine
Überzeugungen, die er mit anderen teilen könnte, nur*

Schlagworte und Ideologien, die er aus den Kommunikationsmedien bezieht.

Er ist zum A-tom geworden (was im Griechischen dem lateinischen Wort »in-dividuum« = unteilbar entspricht), und das einzige Band, das die einzelnen Individuen miteinander verbindet, sind gemeinsame, oft jedoch gleichzeitig antagonistische Interessen und die Verknüpfung durch das Geld.

Emile Durkheim (1897) bezeichnete dieses Phänomen als Anämie, und er hat gefunden, daß es die Hauptursache für den Selbstmord war, der mit der Zunahme der Industrialisierung immer häufiger wurde.

Er verstand unter Anomie die Zerstörung aller traditionellen sozialen Bindungen, die er darauf zurückführte, daß jede echte kollektive Organisation dem Staat gegenüber nur noch eine sekundäre Rolle spielte und daß alles echte soziale Leben verschwunden war. Seiner Ansicht nach waren die im modernen politischen Staat lebenden Menschen »ein desorganisierter Staub von Individuen«."
[Fromm (1989)][29]

---

29 Man needs a social system in which he has his place and in which his relationships with others are relatively stable and supported by generally accepted values and ideas. What has happened in modern industrial society is that traditions, common values and genuine social bonds have largely disappeared.

105

Were the social and moral boundaries too narrow in the Victorian era - are they now too wide? (see also the excursus "Ambivalence of boundaries"). Uncertainty and disorientation are the consequences of too wide boundaries - and can be observed in many cases today.

If one looks at language less as a means of conveying factual information, but rather from a social psychological perspective as both communication of group membership and demarcation from other groups, then the change becomes clear. In the past, villages and places were

---

The modern mass man is isolated and lonely, even when he is part of a crowd; he has no beliefs to share with others, only slogans and ideologies that he gets from the communication media. He has become an atom (which in Greek corresponds to the Latin word "in-dividuum" = indivisible), and the only bond that connects the individuals with each other is common, but often at the same time antagonistic, interests and the connection through money.

Emile Durkheim (1897) called this phenomenon anemia, and he found that it was the main cause of suicide, which became more and more common with the increase in industrialization. He understood anomie as the destruction of all traditional social ties, which he attributed to the fact that any genuine collective organization played only a secondary role compared to the state and that all genuine social life had disappeared. In his view, people living in the modern political state were "a disorganized dust of individuals."

demarcated by dialects that were passed down through generations.

The dialects of young people today, on the other hand, change so quickly that they can hardly be recorded scientifically. The choice of the "Youth Word of the Year" is a desperate attempt that is doomed to failure simply because of the time dimension and regional differences. The language, clothing and "moves" of young people are changing ever faster and at the same time becoming ever more exalted. But they no longer offer orientation and security. On the contrary, the now constantly necessary question of whether one still speaks the right "dialect", still wears the "right" clothes… – and still belongs to the group is unsettling.

7   Results

A construct such as "symbiotic narcissism as a group phenomenon" is only of value if it can be used to describe current problems and processes at all or better and if it can be used to make predictions. So let us now turn to the application of our construct.

7.1.a Excursus: Differentiation between self-confidence and narcissism

In order to understand the construct of "symbiotic narcissism as a group phenomenon", it is necessary to differentiate it from "self-confidence".

So where does self-confidence end and where does narcissism begin?

Social psychology shows, on the one hand, that self-confidence is conveyed through participation in groups, i.e. it does not arise intrapersonally but interpersonally. On the other hand, the need for group membership and maintenance of groups automatically leads to a distinction between in-groups and out-groups, combined with an appreciation of the in-group and a devaluation of out-groups.

„Gleichzeitig ist es vom Standpunkt des Sozialbudgets aus sehr billig, den Gruppennarzißmus zu fördern. Tatsächlich kostet er fast nichts, verglichen mit den Sozialausgaben, die nötig wären, den Lebensstandard zu erhöhen. Die Gesellschaft braucht nur die Ideologen zu bezahlen, die die Schlagworte formulieren, welche den gesellschaftlichen Narzißmus erzeugen. Viele soziale Funktionäre, wie Lehrer, Journalisten, Pfarrer und Professo-

ren, sind zur Mitarbeit bereit, ohne dafür bezahlt zu werden, wenigstens was das Geld anbetrifft. Ihre Belohnung besteht darin, daß sie sich stolz und befriedigt fühlen, einer würdigen Sache zu dienen – und daß ihr Prestige und ihre Aufstiegsmöglichkeiten steigen." [Fromm (1989)][30]

What Fromm describes here is not group narcissism, but the normal manifestation of increasing self-esteem through group participation. But how does "symbiotic narcissism" differ from self-esteem?

It is the difference between a narcissistic-destructive structure on the one hand, and a constructive-(self-)critical one on the other.

The central feature of symbiotic narcissism is therefore not the appreciation of one's own group, which often oc-

---

30 At the same time, from the point of view of the social budget, it is very cheap to promote group narcissism. In fact, it costs almost nothing compared to the social expenditures that would be necessary to raise the standard of living. Society only needs to pay the ideologists who formulate the slogans that generate social narcissism. Many social functionaries, such as teachers, journalists, priests and professors, are willing to cooperate without being paid for it, at least financially. Their reward is that they feel proud and satisfied that they are serving a worthy cause - and that their prestige and opportunities for advancement increase.

curs automatically and unconsciously, but the destructive, static and reality-denying basic structure.

1.22   in communication

The consequences for communication are catastrophic, because it actually comes to a standstill.

A constructive (self-)critical dialogue on the factual level is no longer possible, instead attacks occur primarily on the relationship level.

Your own position and qualifications are ignored just as much as reality. In addition to the collective cries of "We are the people", people are guided by "alternative facts" instead of seeking and perhaps even finding a synthesis through thesis and antithesis.

The arguments are narcissistic and destructive - and shitstorms are the digital manifestation of this.

And it is not without reason that they say:

„The intellectual low-flyers often have communicative air supremacy.“

1.23   in acting in the world

The symbiotic narcissistic structures within groups, with the components described such as ignoring reality and avoiding change..., then lead to, among other things,

1. *pretend help* - fake help that claims to want to help people, but sabotages or ignores everything that would mean help in the sense of positive change. Those who should actually be helped are abused for the purpose of satisfying narcissistic needs.

2. *mutual abuse* - mutual abuse is the result of tolerating "pretend help" from others because you do it yourself. It's like "The Emperor's New Clothes", except that everyone is sometimes a tailor, sometimes an emperor and sometimes a citizen, and therefore always plays along with the others.

3. *bullying* - is the exclusion from a group, either passively as "excommunication" or actively through attacks and hostility.
The consequences for the victim, however, are almost the same.

4. *auto-/destructive behavior* – to satisfy the need for effectiveness while avoiding change and ignoring reality.

5. *intolerance* – towards all people and things that threaten the narcissistic structure.

6. *irrational behavior* - because one does not orient oneself towards reality, but rather perceives reality as threatening.

Terror is therefore the extreme, irrational and (auto)destructive expression of narcissism.

7.1.b   Politics

If one avoids the mistake of "individualizing the irrational" and looks at the manifestations of current political
developments using clinical social psychology, the
symbiotic-narcissistic structures become clear.
Politics also has something of the "unreality" that has
accompanied us from the very beginning in connection
with narcissism.

*„Wenn dagegen in der Menschheitsgeschichte die Domi-
nanz institutionalisiert wird und sich nicht mehr – wie es
noch immer in vielen primitiven Gesellschaften der Fall
ist – eine Funktion der persönlichen Kompetenz ist, dann
ist es nicht mehr notwendig, daß der Führer sich ständig
durch hervorragende Qualität neu auszeichnet, ja, es ist
effektiv nicht einmal nötig, daß er sie überhaupt besitzt.
Das gesellschaftliche System konditioniert die Menschen
dazu, daß sie im Titel, in der Uniform und was es sonst
immer sein mag, den Beweis sehen, daß der Führer kom-
petent ist, und solange diese vom ganzen System
getragenen Symbole vorhanden sind, wird der Durch-
schnittsbürger nicht einmal wagen, sich zu fragen, ob
der Kaiser tatsächlich Kleider anhat."* [Fromm (1989)][31]

---

31   On the other hand, when dominance becomes institutiona-
     lized in human history and no longer a function of personal

Just as it is no longer the best hunters but the best author of a hunting novel who is recognized, in politics it is the person who offers the best apparent solutions.

Political parties, usually equipped with many resources, have a wide range of options to change something concretely, even and especially if they are not elected.

Instead, current politics is characterized not only by an "against" but also by a "we demand!". Unfortunately, constructive (self-)critical approaches are largely lacking. What can be found, however, in the development towards totalitarian regimes, which can be observed in more and more countries, is intolerance towards those who think differently.

„Wer die Wahrheit über ein bestimmtes Regime sagte, ist von den Machthabern, deren Zorn er erregte, von jeher verbannt, ins Gefängnis geworfen oder umgebracht wor-

---

competence, as is still the case in many primitive societies, then it is no longer necessary for the leader to constantly re-exhibit excellence, indeed it is not even necessary for him to possess it at all. The social system conditions people to see in the title, the uniform, and whatever else it may be, proof that the leader is competent, and as long as these symbols, supported by the whole system, are present, the average citizen will not even dare to ask himself whether the emperor really has clothes on.

den. Natürlich lautet die einleuchtende Erklärung dafür, daß solche Menschen dem jeweiligen System gefährlich waren und daß man Status quo am besten schützen konnte, wenn man sie beseitigte. Dies ist nur allzu wahr, doch erklärt es nicht die Tatsache, daß diejenigen, welche die Wahrheit sagen, auch dann so verhaßt sind, wenn sie keine reale Bedrohung der etablierten Ordnung darstellen. Ich glaube, der Grund ist darin zu suchen, daß der, der die Wahrheit sagt, den Widerstand derer mobilisiert, die die Wahrheit verdrängen. Für sie ist die Wahrheit nicht nur deshalb gefährlich, weil sie ihre Macht bedroht, sondern weil sie ihr gesamtes bewußtes Orientierungssystem erschüttert, weil sie sie ihrer Rationalisierungen beraubt und sie sogar zwingen könnte, anders zu handeln. Nur wer diesen Prozeß der Bewußtwerdung wichtiger verdrängter Impulse selbst miterlebt hat, kennt das Gefühl der Bestürzung und Verwirrung, das dieses Erlebnis hervorruft. Nicht jeder ist bereit, dieses Abenteuer zu wagen und am allerwenigsten die, welche wenigstens für den Augenblick von ihrer Blindheit profitieren."
[Fromm (1989)][32]

---

32 Anyone who told the truth about a particular regime has always been banished, imprisoned, or killed by those in power whose anger they aroused. Of course, the obvious explanation is that such people were dangerous to the system in question and that the best way to protect the status

Both destructive and self-destructive behaviors that are characteristic of narcissistic systems also come to light.

„In der politischen Dimension gehören hierzu alle emotional fixierten kollektiven Vorurteilsbildungen gegen Gruppen, Gewohnheiten oder Ideologien, von deren Bekämpfung sich diejenigen eine entscheidende Entlastung von eigenen Schwierigkeiten versprechen, die diesen Vorurteilen unterliegen. Die Betreffenden vernachlässigen eine konstruktive Selbsthilfe, weil sie stereotyp eine

---

quo was to eliminate them. This is all too true, but it does not explain the fact that those who tell the truth are so hated even when they pose no real threat to the established order. I believe the reason is that the person who tells the truth mobilizes the resistance of those who suppress the truth. For them, the truth is dangerous not only because it threatens their power, but because it shakes their entire conscious system of orientation, because it deprives them of their rationalizations and could even force them to act differently.

Only those who have personally experienced this process of becoming aware of important repressed impulses know the feeling of dismay and confusion that this experience evokes. Not everyone is prepared to risk this adventure, least of all those who benefit from their blindness, at least for the moment.

Erlösung von ihren Problemen durch Unschädlichma-
chung der bösen äußeren Einflüsse erwarten. "
[Richter (1982)][33]

The calls for borders and walls, for exclusion and depor-
tation, for defense against external influences, are becoming louder and louder.

7.1.c   Splitting of communities

The narcissistic and destructive conflict is creating a problem whose extent cannot yet be estimated. There are
almost no repairable rifts in societies, for example with
Erdogan, Brexit, Trump... opponents on one side and supporters on the other.
And the "communicative" processes of the conflict are so
catastrophic that it doesn't really matter what or for
whom the decision is made, e.g. in the form of an election. The structure of societies is largely and irreconcilably

---

33 In the political dimension, this includes all emotionally
     fixed collective prejudices against groups, habits or ideolo-
     gies, which those who are subject to these prejudices hope
     will provide a decisive relief from their own problems. The
     people concerned neglect constructive self-help because
     they stereotypically expect to be relieved of their problems
     by neutralizing the evil external influences.

destroyed. There are hostile and irreconcilable camps facing each other, between which the bridges of communication have been destroyed. Between which there is no longer any discourse, indeed, due to the denial of both reality and change, no discourse can even take place.

We find ourselves in a post-factual society that is largely characterized by (antagonistic) symbiotic-narcissistic structures. The prognosis for such a social structure is also not very good due to the (auto)destructive tendencies, the elements that ignore reality and fear change.
We therefore very much hope that we are wrong in our portrayal of "symbiotic narcissism as a group phenomenon". In any case, the necessary establishment of "clinical social psychology" remains untouched.

117

BIBLIOGRAPHY

Adler, Alfred (1977): Über den nervösen Charakter. Grundzüge einer vergleichenden Individual-Psychotherapie. Frankfurt/M.

Agroskin, Dmitrij; Klackl, Johannes; Jonas, Eva; Siegel, Allan (2014): The Self-Liking Brain. A VBM Study on the Structural Substrate of Self-Esteem. In: *PLoS ONE* 9 (1), e86430.

Bargh, John A. (2014): Social psychology and the unconscious. The automaticity of higher mental processes. New York: Psychology Press

Bronfenbrenner, Urie (1977): Toward an experimental ecology of human development. In: *American Psychologist* 32 (7), S. 513–531.

Bronfenbrenner, Urie (1986): Ecology of the Family as a Context for Human Development: Research Perspectives. In: *Developmental Psychology* (23), S. 723–742.

Bronfenbrenner, Urie (1995): Developmental Ecology Through Space and Time: A Future Perspective.

Bronfenbrenner_&_Ceci_ (1994): Nature-Nurture Reconceptualized Developmental Perspective: A Biological Model. In: *Psychological Review* 1994 (101), S. 568–586.

Dunning, David (2012): Self-insight. Roadblocks and detours on the path to knowing thyself. 3rd print. New York: Psychology Press

Fromm, Erich (1989): Gesamtausgabe. 1. Aufl., 1. [Dr.]. München: Dt. Taschenbuch-Verl. (VII).

Ganz, Andreas; Schmidt, Bernhard J. (2016): Klartext kompakt. Frühkindlicher Autismus: Verstehen = Helfen. Norderstedt

Haun, Daniel B. M.; Tomasello, Michael (2011): Conformity to Peer Pressure in Preschool Children. In: *Child Development* 82 (6),

Hoyningen-Huene, Paul (2013): Systematicity. The nature of science. New York: Oxford University Press

Lasch, Christopher (1980): Das Zeitalter des Narzißmus. München: Steinhausen.

Leary, Mark R. (2002): The Interpersonal Basis of Self-Esteem. In: Joseph P. Forgas und Kipling D. Williams (Hg.): The Social Self: Cognitive, Interpersonal and Intergroup Perspectives // The social self.

Le Bon, Gustave (1895/2016): Psychologie der Massen. Unter Mitarbeit von Rudolf Eisler. Köln: Anaconda Verlag.

Leyens, Jacques-Philippe; Cortes, Brezo; Demoulin, Stephanie; Dovidio, John F.; Fiske, Susan T.; Gaunt, Ruth et al. (2003): Emotional prejudice, essentialism, and nationalism The 2002 Tajfel lecture. In: *Eur. J. Soc. Psychol.* 33 (6), S. 703–717. DOI: 10.1002/ejsp.170.

Lowen, Alexander (1992): Narzissmus. Die Verleugnung des wahren Selbst. 1. Aufl. München: Goldmann (Goldmann, 12314).

Lumsden, Joanne; Miles, Lynden K.; Macrae, C. Neil (2014): Sync or sink? Interpersonal synchrony impacts self-esteem. In: *Front. Psychol.* 5 (164), S. 96. DOI: 10.3389/fpsyg.2014.01064.

Menzies Lyth, Isabel (1960): Social Systems as a Defense Against Anxiety. An Empirical Study of the Nursing Service of a General Hospital. In: Human Relations (13), S. 95–121.

Milgram, Stanley; Fleissner, Roland (2015): Das Milgram-Experiment. Zur Gehorsamsbereitschaft gegenüber Autorität. 19. Auflage. Reinbek bei Hamburg: Rowohlt (Rororo, 17479. Sachbuch).

Postman, Neil (1994): Wir amüsieren uns zu Tode. Urteilsbildung im Zeitalter der Unterhaltungsindustrie. 7. Aufl. Frankfurt am Main: Fischer

Richter, Horst-Eberhard (1982): Der Gotteskomplex. D. Geburt u.d. Krise d. Glaubens an d. Allmacht d. Menschen. 81. - 85. Tsd. Reinbek bei Hamburg: Rowohlt.

Schmidt, Bernhard J. (2015/1): Autist und Gesellschaft - Ein zorniger Perspektivenwechsel. Band 1: Autismus verstehen. Norderstedt

Schmidt, Bernhard J. (2015/2): Autist und Gesellschaft - Ein zorniger Perspektivenwechsel. Band 2: Hilfen für Autisten? 1. Aufl. Norderstedt

Schmidt, Bernhard J. (2016): Autismus. Wenn Händewaschen hilft. Norderstedt

Schmidt, Bernhard J. (2017): Autismus und der Kühlschrankmutter Mythos. Eine Rehabilitierung Bruno Bettelheims. 1. Auflage.

Schmidt, Bernhard J.; Ganz, Andreas (2016): KLARTEXT KOMPAKT. Das Asperger Syndrom - nicht nur für Psychotherapeuten.

Smith, Peter B.; Bond, Michael Harris (1998): Social psychology across cultures. 2. ed., 6. pr. Harlow [u.a.], Harlow [u.a.]: Prentice Hall Europe.

Thomas, Alexander (1991): Grundriß der Sozialpsychologie. Göttingen: Verl. für Psychologie Hogrefe.

Thomas, Alexander (1998): Individuum, Gruppe, Gesellschaft. [S.l.]: [s.n.] (Grundriss der Sozialpsychologie / Alexander Thomas, Bd. 2).

Vaihinger, Hans (1920): Die Philosopie des Als Ob. System der theoretischen, praktischen und religiösen Fiktionen der Menschheit auf Grund eines idealistischen Positivismus: Felix Meiner.

Vygotskij, Lev Semenovič (1929); in Rieber, Robert W.; Carton, Aaron S. (op. 1987-): The collected works of L.S. Vygotsky. New York: Plenum Press (Cognition and language).

Wenger, Etienne (1998): Communities of practice. Learning, meaning, and identity. Cambridge: Cambridge University Press

Wetherell, Margaret (1996): Social psychology. Personnal lives, social worlds. London, Thousand Oaks, Calif.: Sage Publications in association with the Open University.

Yafai, Abdul-Fattah; Verrier, Diarmuid; Reidy, Lisa (2014): Social conformity and autism spectrum disorder: a child-friendly take on a classic study. In: *Autism : the international journal of research and practice* 18 (8), S. 1007–1013. DOI: 10.1177/1362361313508023.

Zimbardo, Philip G. (1972): The Pathology of Imprisonment. Online: http://www.vonsteuben.org/ourpages/auto/2013/9/16/39586652/Zimbardo%20Pathology%20of%20Imprisonment.pdf